# Derry at Pl

## Memories of the Theatre Club anc

Gerry Downey

**Gerry (front left) and his flatmate Peter Gallagher (third left at back) are pictured here with several members of the Queen's University Cumann Gaelach and other friends, enjoying an Easter trip to Donegal. The group includes the young Bellaghy poet Seamus Heaney, who would later remember the week in his poem The Gaeltacht. Thirty years later, Gerry and 'Big Peadar' would go on to set up the North West Institute's Performing Arts Academy.**

# PROLOGUE: LOVE IN A COLD CLIMATE

My father Gerry was a born performer.

He loved nothing better than the roar of his greasepaint and the smell of the crowd. And, as fortune would have it, he was good at it – and had a memory like Shylock to boot.

Up until recently, given the least possible provocation, he would recite (or act out) entire scenes by Shakespeare or Molière or Friel, or poems from Ó Raifteirí and Frost and his old St Columb's friend Seamus Heaney. But about thirty years ago he noticed it was becoming harder to retain new scripts, so he began to shy away from bigger stage parts in favour of production, teaching and the odd bit of filming, (which he loved).

His last major stage role was at the Derry Playhouse in the early 2000s in Yabo Yablonsky's New York street-gangs biodrama Jews Without Money, during which he had to execute a terrifyingly-intricate, five-minute-long soliloquy. Yabo, best known for his Hollywood film Escape to Victory, was directing the Playhouse production and inspired a spellbinding performance from Gerry, who – to this untrained eye at least – stole the show.

As a younger cynic, it was hard to fathom my father's motivation. Why would anyone spend months learning lines, or coaching others, only to perform in front of a maximum of 100 people in the Little Theatre - much fewer again when there were roadblocks, power strikes, riots and bombings? Likewise, it was difficult to understand the Herculean effort the Theatre Club put into productions that could only run for a few nights, or the pride it took in its work in a world that was often disintegrating around it.

Shortly before his death in 2020, I asked club founder Seán McMahon what had driven him to persist so stubbornly with amateur productions in the middle of a war, with no prospect of thanks, gain or even recognition. He deliberated carefully before explaining that they did it because they wanted to entertain audiences and give them a release; that it was their tradition and their duty. But most of all, they did it because they could do no other.

"The word amateur derives from the Latin for love," he said, "and people like your father and I were true amateurs, who genuinely loved what we were doing. We had to do it. It was in us."

My younger brother Rónán, of course, never had to be told any of this. Just as with Gerry, it was in him from day one.

At a tender age, Rónán befriended Jennifer Johnston, while acting in the screen adaptation of her novel Shadows on our Skin, before going on to star alongside Liam Neeson and Eleanor Bron in the coming-of-age film My Dear Palestrina. (The family legend about Neeson is that Gerry had to give him a lift to the Guildhall one evening and borrowed my mother Áine's tiny Fiat 126 for the job. He claims he had to fold Neeson into the seat, jam his knees against the dashboard and bust open the sunroof: 'I'd a' been better giving him a bar on me bike...' Bron, meanwhile doted on Rónán and, according to Áine, had to be physically restrained from adopting him.)

A few years ago, Gerry suggested someone should compile a scrapbook of the Theatre Club's golden era before it slipped from the communal memory and, as was becoming apparent, his own. He began putting together a few of his old programmes and notes. And, as his forgetfulness began to progress, I sounded out a couple of former club stalwarts to see if they might have the time to chip in. But they had such busy lives it felt unfair to impose.

Then a few months ago, Gerry's brother John handed me a small pile of Theatre Club memorabilia he had found in my father's old boxes. And tag, I was it.

A 'Derry Theatre Club retro' Facebook page was the next step, which led back to the Ryder family, to Jean Flaherty (who knows me from pre-birth – she had taught with my mother Áine at St Mary's in the 1960s), the McMahon family, Terry Willman, Billy Gallagher, Gerry McAuley, the Toals, the Craigs, Mairead Mullan, Connor Porter, Art Byrne, the Gillen family, Clann Mhic Gabhann, the Cunninghams, the Boyles, Joe Mahon, Maeve Connelly, Joe Martin and a host of other old friends, who helped out greatly.

It also led back into prehistory and our players' origin stories; to numerous other North West drama groups; to the Theatre Action Group and its hard-fought campaign for purpose-built performance space; to the Faces of Ireland series; to professional theatre with Field Day; to Derry's emerging broadcast and film sectors; to the Journal's magnificently curated archive, (thank you, yet again, Sean McLaughlin); to Jenni Doherty at Little Acorns Bookstore, and Ken Thatcher at Foyle Books; down many rabbit-holes, and otherwise to the end of the internet and back.

So the final result is a peculiar animal – not quite a horse as drawn by committee, more perhaps a lumpy little elephant, drawn from Gerry's own experiences.

It is an unfinished elephant, missing legs, tusks and ears, no doubt. It is certainly not a definitive history. But we hope it can evoke some memories of those determined and talented players, who spent so many evenings lighting their candles to ward off the darkness - and provide us in the stalls with such happy times.

Derry Theatre Club, 1970 to 1994: the pleasure was all ours.

Garbhán Downey, October 2022

The Mortons Who Spoke Chinese
A Family Memoir
Áine Downey

**Gerry's is the second Downey memoir to be published by Colmcille Press in recent years, following Áine's nostalgic account of her childhood in the only Irish-speaking family in East Belfast in the '40s and '50s.**

Ronan Downey, Crawford Square. 24TLS56.

# RONAN LANDS PART IN PLAY

A 12 year old Londonderry boy, Ronan Downey, of Crawford Square, has been cast for a part in the BBC play 'The Last Palestrina' by Bernard McLaverty which is due to go into rehearsals on June 16.

A pupil of St. Columb's College, Ronan was one of six Londonderry boys who were auditioned for part of Danny in the play, which is set in a Northern Ireland village in the 1950s.

•

FILMING

Danny, the central character, is a musically-talented boy, and the role of the music-teacher will be played by Eleanor Bron. The executive producer will be Neil Zeiger.

Filming in the studio and on location will commence on July 7.

Gerry's son Rónán, 1968-2000, was a natural, featuring in Derek Mahon's screen adaptation of Jennifer Johnston's novel Shadows on our Skin, and starring in the BBC's My Dear Palestrina, alongside Eleanor Bron and Liam Neeson.

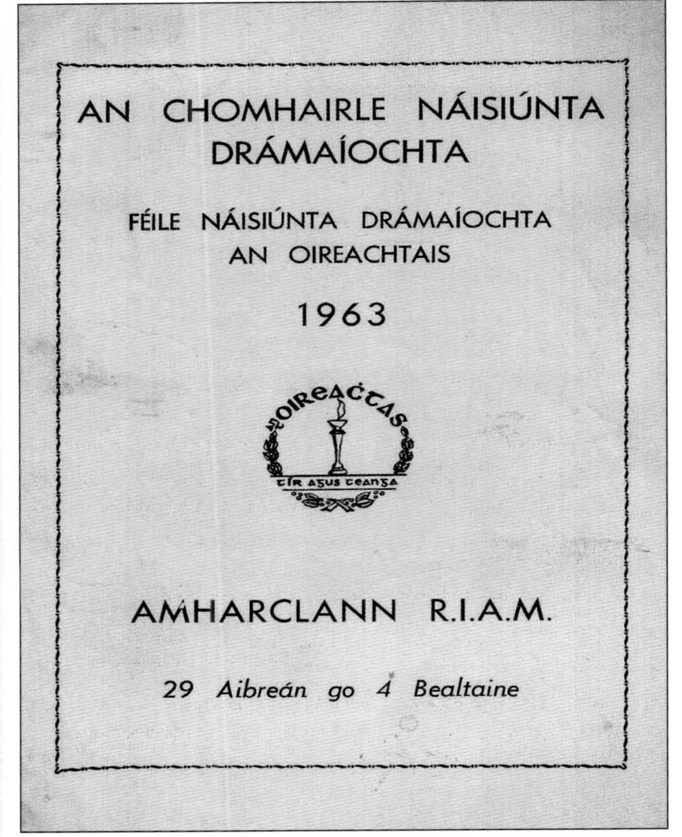

AN CHOMHAIRLE NÁISIÚNTA DRÁMAÍOCHTA

FÉILE NÁISIÚNTA DRÁMAÍOCHTA AN OIREACHTAIS

1963

OIREACHTAS

TÍR AGUS TEANGA

AMHARCLANN R.I.A.M.

*29 Aibreán go 4 Bealtaine*

**Dé Sathairn, 7 p.m.** **4 Bealtaine, 19963**

**AN SÉÚ SEISIÚN**

**11. Aisteoirí na Rinne, Rinn ó gCuanach** : "Nemesis" leis an Athair Victor de Paor. (Ainmnithe ó Fhéile na Mumhan).

Foireann

Bean a' Tí ... ... ... ... Gile Ní Fhoghlú
Muiris, ... ... ... ... Tomás de Faoite
An Stróinséar ... ... ... ... Parthalán Breathnach

*Léiritheoir* : An tAthair Victor de Paor

**12. An Cumann Gaelach, Ollscoil na Ríona, Béal Feirste** : "Lá Fhéile Michíl"—duaisdráma ó Oireachtas 1962 le Eoghan Ó Tuairisc. (Ainmnithe ó Fhéile Uladh).

*Radharc* : Gáirdín Chlochair.

*Am* : Meán Fómhair, 1922.

*Réamhradharc* : Breacadh an Lae.

Gníomh I ... ... Maidin.
Gníomh II ... ... Iarnóin.
Gníomh III ... ... Tráthnóna.

Foireann

An Mháthair Oirmhinneach ... ... Déirdre Ní Fhrighil
Máistreás na Nuasachán ... ... ... Áine Ní Mhaoláin
Nuala de Búrca (Nuasachán) ... ... Áine Ní Riain
Maesi Ní Mhuireagáin (Nuasachán eile) ... Isibéal Nic Ghiolla Riabhaigh
An Sagart Mór ... ... ... ... Risteard Skerett
An Sagart Óg ... ... ... ... Eoghan Ó Cromtha
Emmet de Búrca ... ... ... ... Annraoi Ó Preith
Pacai Armstrong ... ... ... ... Pádraig Mac Duinnshléibhe
Murtach (Garradóir) ... ... ... Seoirse Champkin
Teachtaire ... ... ... ... Gearóid Mac Giolla Domhnaigh

*Léiritheoir* : Lionard Ó Coigligh

**13. Conradh na Gaeilge, Lonndain, 99 Belgrave Rd., Victoria, S.W.1.**: "Cruadh-chás na mBaitsiléirí" le Úna Bean Uí Dhiosca.

*Radharc* : Gáirdín.

Foireann

Seán ... ... ... ... ... Seán Ó Rafartaigh
Liam ... ... ... ... ... Seán Ó Laoghaire
Caitlín ... ... ... ... ... Eibhlín Ní Churráin
Gráinne ... ... ... ... ... Máire Ní Ruairc

*Léiritheoir* : Seán Ó Laoghaire

The Queen's Cumann Gaelach are winners in the 1963 annual Oireachtas Irish Language National Theatre Festival. Gerry plays a messenger (teachtaire) in the Eoghan Ó Tuairisc play Lá Fhéile Michíl – and jots the scores on his programme.

The talented amateur actor Joey Glover, whose killing will send a shockwave through Derry's theatrical circles and also the city as a whole.

THEATRE CLUB

presents

"The Death and Resurrection of Mr. Roche"

By Thomas Kilroy.

City Hotel

8p.m. Monday, 9th November '70

The Derry-born dramatist George Farquhar (1677-1707), who started it all. He is commemorated with a Blue Plaque at the Verbal Arts Centre, and a studio is named after him at the Millennium Forum.

Several of the cast from this St Columb's College Past Pupils Union production of The Importance of Being Earnest will go on to become Theatre Club performers, including Eamonn Gallagher, Bridget Keenan, Michael Gillen and Tony McKeown. Dympna Armstrong's young sister Anita (Robinson) will become the company's wardrobe mistress. Anita will later reference the club in her memoir, Twice Around on the Hobby Horse (Brehon Press, 2007).

# ACT ONE:
# BIRTHING PAINS

*(A group of young players searches for a home.)*

Derry's Theatre Club was certainly in existence by 1970 but was possibly conceived earlier. The company accounts indicate that before Lovers, the club's first stage production in February 1971, the players had hosted seven rehearsed readings in the previous financial year: Step in the Hollow; The Playboy of the Western World; The Importance of Being Earnest; The Death and Resurrection of Mr Roche; The House of Bernarda Alba; Long Day's Journey into Night; and Philadelphia Here I Come.

The Theatre Club would go on to produce forty-four stage plays over the next fourteen years, and at least another 18 that we can trace before winding down in 1994, though no definitive record seems to exist.

As an incubator, the club would have few equals. It would have a profound impact not just on the North West drama scene but also across the island and across the globe. Its long-standing friend Brian Friel would go on to conquer Broadway; producer Jennifer Johnston would win international awards for her novels; while other young recruits would go on to become filmmakers, broadcasters, writers and musicians of great renown.

The club's first surviving programme dates from November 9, 1970, for the reading of Tom Kilroy's Death and Resurrection of Mr Roche. This event took place opposite the Guildhall at the old City Hotel, at the time one of Derry's most prestigious venues. (It was blown up in May 1972 and never rebuilt.) Clareman Art Byrne was producer for the night; the players were Byrne himself, Sean 'Barlow' Cassidy, Gerry Downey, Eddie Mailey, Seán McMahon, Dinah Sinton and Barney Toal; and they took £2.70 at the door. Even in 1970, that was not a lot of money.

It was Seán McMahon – a driving force behind the club from its instigation – who saw the need to find a home for the players, and he approached Father Edward Daly (later Bishop) to ask for use of what would become known as the Little Theatre on Orchard Street. The facility was a 100-seat former minor hall, downstairs and around the corner from the much grander 900-seat St Columb's Hall, owned by the church.

McMahon made it clear to Daly from the outset that he could not expect script approval before performances, something the church was demanding in other parts of the island at that time. Sligo-born Jean Flaherty remembers as a student in Galway scripts being returned by a priest with full sections scored out with blue pen – in one case, an entire one-act play was struck out.

Daly, however, was a genuine supporter of the arts and gave the Theatre Club fair wind, and he rented them the Little Theatre. A short time afterwards, however, the young priest did set up another troupe, the 71 Players, which would also use the theatre. And whilst there was a perceived rivalry between the groups – some of the Theatre Club might have fancied themselves as intellectuals, and the "78 Players" were all about filling houses – there was, in reality, great respect

**Lifelong dramatist and Theatre Club founder Seán McMahon, with his sleeves rolled up for business, in rehearsals for Oklahoma in 1955.**

between the groups and they would support the other's productions.

A significant portion of the Theatre Club's early membership, including its first chair Bridget Keenan, would have come from the North West's other drama groups, many of which stopped performing because of the Troubles. Pre-1969, there was a lively amateur scene in the city, which included: St Columb's College Past Pupils Union, the Convent of Mercy (later Thornhill) PPU, the Londonderry Drama Society, the Londonderry Amateur Operatic Society (LAOS), the Londonderry Musical Society, the YMCA Players, the City of Derry Drama Club (CDDC), the Tower Players, An Craobh, the Colmcille Players, the Foyle Players, the Kieran Players, the Green Circle, and St Enda's D.S. There were also regular drama festivals, for adults and students, in Derry, West Tyrone and Inishowen.

But the conflict made life difficult, if not nigh impossible, for theatre. Touring groups stopped visiting the city, and audiences for those who did make the journey were dropping. Festivals were cancelled, and producers became more and more risk averse. Performers and audiences were too frightened to leave home.

During one particular Theatre Club play, set in war-torn Europe, the script dictated several offstage explosions be included as 'noises off', so cuing up lines and scenes. But on performance night, Derry was rocked with a series of bombs louder than anything the players' sound engineer could ever produce.

"It was crazy when you look back, but we laughed at [the irony of] it," said one actor. The same player, however, recalls the devastation felt by the troupe when they went across to 'Peter Owenses' for a Christmas pint after a show in 1972 to learn that six patrons had been massacred in an attack on a pub just a few hundred yards away on the other side of the bridge.

In her book From Farquhar to Field Day: Three Centuries of Music and Theatre in Derry~Londonderry, (History Press Ireland, 2012), Nuala McAllister Hart catalogued how the town, to quote Phil Coulter, was "brought to its knees".

Groups like the Operatic Society, St Columb's Cathedral Music Society, and Feis Dhoire suspended activities; others like the Britannia Band were forced into closure as members couldn't attend practice sessions in the city centre. The City of Derry Drama Club, meanwhile, lost all its equipment in a malicious fire, forcing it to shut down.

The Guildhall, the city's number one venue, was bombed twice in 1972 rendering it unusable, leaving Magee's Great Hall as the city's last remaining prestige facility. And in 1976, the murder of one of the town's most popular amateur performers, Joey Glover, would shake the North West drama community to its core.

It was by no means an easy beginning.

EVEN THE VIOLENT UNCERTAINTY of Derry's darkest days failed to extinguish the flame of the arts. Groups like the Theatre Club and the '71 Players continued to stage productions where the cast sometimes outnumbered the audience. Ah, the joys of amateur dramatics! All over the province rehearsals are in full swing for everything from *Boyd's Shop* to Beckett. Even as we speak, there are people out there not able to eat a bite at the imminent prospect of stepping onstage at 8pm in an ill-fitting wig and somebody else's shoes. Amnesiac with anxiety their one thought is "People are paying to see this!"

**Anita Robinson salutes the Theatre Club in her memoir, Twice Around on the Hobby Horse (Brehon Press, 2007).**

**Fr Edward Daly (later Bishop) founder of the 71 Players, with Neil McMahon and James McCafferty.**

**Ireland's greatest actress Siobhan McKenna travels to Derry in June 1972 to guest-star in a one-off reprise of 'Cass McGuire'. The photo shows Shantallow Festival Queen Frances Campbell (later Eurovision contestant with Sheeba and BBC radio presenter) presenting a bouquet of flowers to McKenna as Theatre Club members look on. From left are Deirdre McGinley, Terry Willman, Eddie Mailey, Kevin McLaughlin, Gerry Downey, Phillippa Russell, Bernard Toal (producer) and Bart O'Donnell. The picture appears on the front page of the Derry Journal. Following the after-show party, Ms McKenna, who by all accounts is a determined woman, visits the Bogside Inn with the mission of persuading the then-feuding Provos and Stickies to bury the hatchet. Her impassioned plea to the gallery, however, only manages to spark a 'full Wild West' riot in the bar and Gerry has to bundle Ireland's greatest stage actress into a (safe) waiting car. Derry is clearly not ready for McKenna whose one-woman show at the Lourdes Hall in the Brandywell fails to draw a crowd. At curtain up, when producer Fr Denis Bradley is advised to scrap the few bob entrance fee and allow free entry to the show, he retorts: "I already announced it an hour ago..."**

"deprived as our city is at present of every kind of public entertainment, the operations of the proposed society could not fail to give a fixed intellectual bias to the public taste"—londonderry natural history society (1838). following the precedent of our forefathers, we issue a brief prospectus. we would like to attempt some of the best modern european and american plays. and we would also like to bring modern irish plays here as soon as possible after their professional productions. many of these plays will not attract audiences large enough to fill the bigger halls. and, in any case, much is lost in such halls, given the limited abilities of amateur actors. what derry needs is a small hall, holding 100 - 300 people, with stage, lighting and a raked auditorium—in short a little theatre. our present venue is not such a theatre. a refurnished minor hall in orchard street may come nearer to filling the need. but the eventual answer would be a properly designed civic theatre. and as such a theatre would be neither 'sanctified' nor forced to play an old austrian tune; all citizens could frequent it with their principles intact.

PRINTED BY L.H.S. PRESS

**theatre club presents**

**lovers**

**by brian friel**

on 25/26/27 february 1971

in the union hall, shipquay st.

at 8.00 p.m.

**admission 25p. [by programme]**

**friday**

№ 000005

**The Union Hall at the bottom corner of Shipquay Street inside the walls is the venue for the first full Theatre Club production. The programme, which costs 25p and serves as your admission ticket, also features the club's manifesto.**

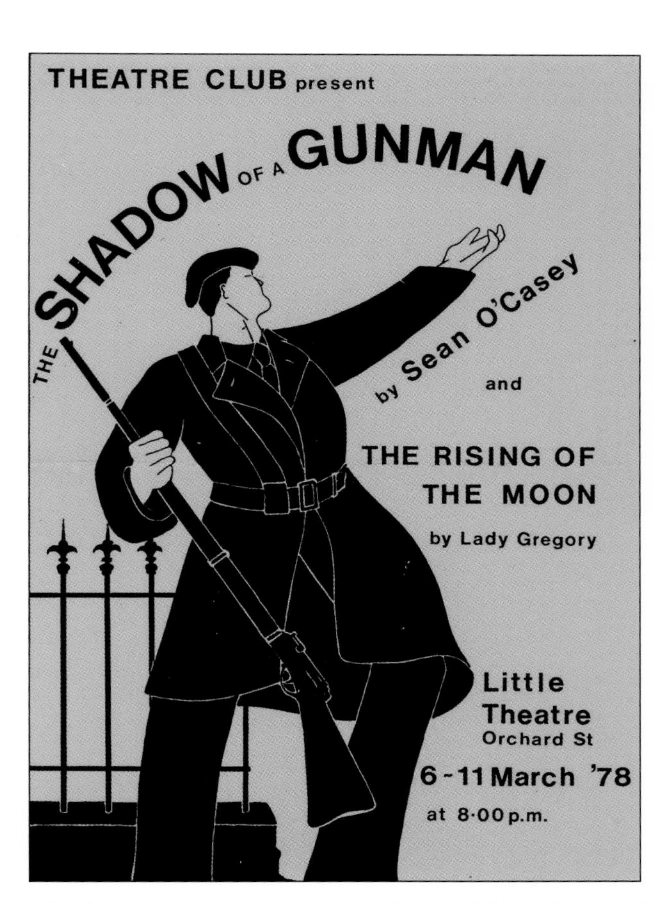


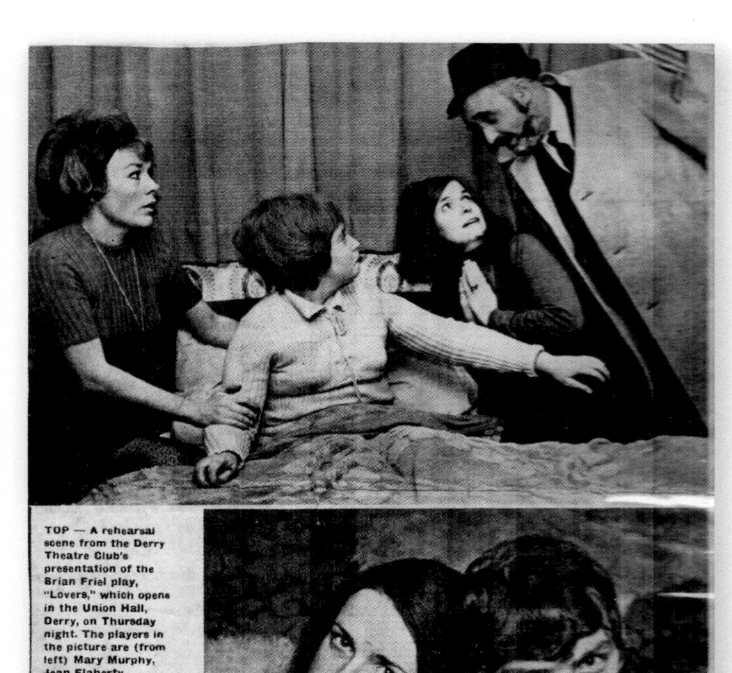

TOP — A rehearsal scene from the Derry Theatre Club's presentation of the Brian Friel play, "Lovers," which opens in the Union Hall, Derry, on Thursday night. The players in the picture are (from left) Mary Murphy, Jean Flaherty, Philippa Russell and Bernard Toal.

RIGHT — "Lovers" is really two plays. The first is called "Winners" and the second "Losers." In "Winners" there are only two players — Paula Toal and Ian Doherty.

**Clippings and programmes from the Theatre Club's early years. The cast list for Men Without Shadows is allegedly larger than the audiences. It is the last time the club will ever attempt to perform Sartre.**

THEATRE CLUB PRESENTS

# MEN WITHOUT SHADOWS

In November 1946, "Morts sans sepulture" opened. Sartre had written thisplay before; at the time when the ex-collaborators were beginning to show themselves again, he had wanted to refresh people's memories. He had thought a great deal about torture for four whole years; alone, and among friends, he asked himself: Should I not speak about it too? What would be the best way to handle it? He had also pondered a great deal on the relation between the torturer and his victim. All these thoughts that haunted him he threw into his play. Once more he confronted ethics and "praxis": Lucie retreats stubbornly into her individualistic pride, while the militant Communist, presented by Sartre as in the right, aims at effectiveness.

Vitold was to direct. But it hadn't been easy finding a producer and a theatre. The torture scene scared people off. Finally Simone Berriau, who had just taken on the Theatre Antoine again, accepted it. Masson did the scenery.

The tortures in "Morts sans sepulture" took place almost entirely behind the scenery; seen from the wings they weren't very frightening, and even made us laugh, since the martyr, Vitold, always famished at that hour, would hurl himself on a sandwich as soon as he got off stage and bolt it between shrieks. On opening night I was in the audience and everything changed. I had experienced before the process by which a game without consequence is transformed into an event; but this time, as the cautious theatre managers had predicted, the fruit of this metamorphasis was a scandal. It even affected me; hearing them with the ears of the other spectators, Vitold's shrieks were almost intolerable. Mme. Steve Passeur stood up and shouted, very straight underneath her hat: "It's a disgrace." In the orchestra people even came to blows. Aron's wife left at the intermission, having almost fainted, and he followed her. The meaning of this uproar was clear: the bourgeoisie was initiating a re-unification, and to awaken such unpleasant memories seemed the height of bad taste.

The Communists, generally speaking, supported "Morts sans sepulture." Yet when Sartre saw Ehrenburg for the first time, he reproached him bitterly for having depicted the members of the Resistance as cowards and traitors. Sartre couldn't believe his ears. "Have you read the play?" Ehrenburg admitted that he had only skimmed through the first scene or two. "If I got that impression, there must have been reason for it." The Communists' conception of what literature should be was very rigidly fixed, a grievance was he wouldn't comply to it.

*Simone de Beauvoir: "Force of Circumstance"*

LITTLE THEATRE 23rd—27th May, 1972

Produced by ART BYRNE

| | |
|---|---|
| RANCOIS | ROBIN PEOPLES |
| ORBIER | BOB McKIMM |
| ANORIS | EDDIE MAILEY |
| UCIE | ANNE O'LEARY |
| ENRI | SEAN McMAHON |
| EAN | JIM CRAIG |
| ANDRIEU | PETER MULLAN |
| ELLERIN | TERENCE O'BRIEN |
| LOCHET | FRANK O'KANE |
| ILITIAMAN | TOM HAVERTY |

| | |
|---|---|
| Production Assistant | JEAN FLAHERTY |
| Stage Manager | CHRIS TROTTER |
| Sets and Lighting designed by | DAVID NOBLE |
| Lighting Assistant | GEORGE McDOWELL |
| Stage Assistant | JACKIE McCAULEY |
| Make-up | NEIL McMAHON |
| Publicity | GERRY McLAUGHLIN |
| Business Manager | The Secretary, MISS P. BOYLE, 5 LAWRENCE HILL. TEL. 2053. |

INTERVAL OF 20 MINUTES AFTER ACT 1 SCENE 2.

PATRONS ARE REQUESTED NOT TO SMOKE IN THE THEATRE.

PRODUCTIONS:–

| | | |
|---|---|---|
| 1970 - 71 | | |
| February | LOVERS | Brian Friel |
| May | THE QUEEN AND THE REBELS | Ugo Betti |
| 1971 - 72 | | |
| October | THE LOVES OF CASS McGUIRE | Brian Friel |
| December | STEPHEN D | Hugh Leonard |
| April | THE PROMISE | Aleksei Arbuzov |
| May | MEN WITHOUT SHADOWS | Jean-Paul Sartre |

The Theatre Club thanks all their patrons and the Management of the Little Theatre who have helped to make last year such a success. We also thank the many business houses who have aided us financially by advertising in our programmes.

Programme designed by David Noble and printed by Nu-Print Ltd.

**David Noble was a creative genius. His programmes and posters were works of art in themselves.**

Members of the Derry Theatre Club pictured during rehearsals for their presentation of Brian Friel's "Lovers," which will be staged in the Union Hall, Derry, commencing next Wednesday night. From left —Sean McMahon (producer), Jean Flaherty ("Mrs. Wilson"), Phillipa Russell ("Cissie Cassidy"), Bernard Toal ("Andy Tracey"), and Mary Murphy ("Hannah Wilson").

**Broadway playwright Hugh Leonard (aka Jack Byrne) proves a big supporter of the Theatre Club, writing the programme notes for this Theatre Club production of The Poker Session, pictured above, starring Thelma Arthur, Noleen Taylor, Jean Flaherty, Sean McMahon, Bob McKimm and Declan O'Kelly.**

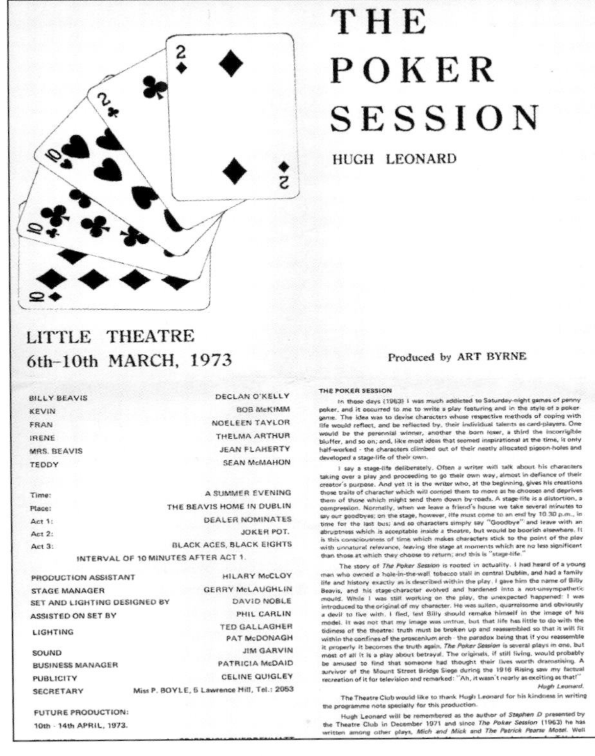

THE POKER SESSION

HUGH LEONARD

LITTLE THEATRE
6th–10th MARCH, 1973

Produced by ART BYRNE

| | |
|---|---|
| BILLY BEAVIS | DECLAN O'KELLY |
| KEVIN | BOB McKIMM |
| FRAN | NOELEEN TAYLOR |
| IRENE | THELMA ARTHUR |
| MRS. BEAVIS | JEAN FLAHERTY |
| TEDDY | SEAN McMAHON |

| | |
|---|---|
| Time: | A SUMMER EVENING |
| Place: | THE BEAVIS HOME IN DUBLIN |
| Act 1: | DEALER NOMINATES |
| Act 2: | JOKER POT. |
| Act 3: | BLACK ACES, BLACK EIGHTS |

INTERVAL OF 10 MINUTES AFTER ACT 1.

| | |
|---|---|
| PRODUCTION ASSISTANT | HILARY McCLOY |
| STAGE MANAGER | GERRY McLAUGHLIN |
| SET AND LIGHTING DESIGNED BY | DAVID NOBLE |
| ASSISTED ON SET BY | PHIL CARLIN |
| LIGHTING | TED GALLAGHER<br>PAT McDONAGH |
| SOUND | JIM GARVIN |
| BUSINESS MANAGER | PATRICIA McDAID |
| PUBLICITY | CELINE QUIGLEY |
| SECRETARY | Miss P. BOYLE, 5 Lawrence Hill, Tel.: 2053 |

FUTURE PRODUCTION:
10th - 14th APRIL, 1973.

THE POKER SESSION

In those days (1963) I was much addicted to Saturday-night games of penny poker, and it occurred to me to write a play featuring and in the style of a poker game. The idea was to devise characters whose respective methods of coping with life would reflect, and be reflected by, their individual talents as card-players. One would be the perennial winner, another the born loser, a third the incorrigible bluffer, and so on; and, like most ideas that seemed inspirational at the time, it only half-worked - the characters climbed out of their neatly allocated pigeon-holes and developed a stage-life of their own.

I say a stage-life deliberately. Often a writer will talk about his characters taking over a play and proceeding to go their own way, almost in defiance of their creator's purpose. And yet it is the writer who, at the beginning, gives his creations those traits of character which will compel them to move as he chooses and deprives them of those which might send them down by-roads. A stage-life is a distortion, a compression. Normally, when we leave a friend's house we take several minutes to say our goodbyes; on the stage, however, life must come to an end by 10.30 p.m., in time for the last bus; and so characters simply say "Goodbye" and leave with an abruptness which is acceptable inside a theatre, but would be boorish elsewhere. It is this consciousness of time which makes characters stick to the point of the play with unnatural relevance, leaving the stage at moments which are no less significant than those at which they choose to return; and this is "stage-life."

The story of *The Poker Session* is rooted in actuality. I had heard of a young man who owned a hole-in-the-wall tobacco stall in central Dublin, and had a family life and history exactly as is described within the play. I gave him the name of Billy Beavis, and his stage-character evolved and hardened into a not-unsympathetic mould. While I was still working on the play, the unexpected happened: I was introduced to the original of my character. He was sullen, quarrelsome and obviously a devil to live with. I fled, lest Billy should remake himself in the image of his model. It was not that my image was untrue, but that life has little to do with the tidiness of the theatre: truth must be broken up and reassembled so that it will fit within the confines of the proscenium arch - the paradox being that if you reassemble it properly it becomes the truth again. *The Poker Session* is several plays in one, but most of all it is a play about betrayal. The originals, if still living, would probably be amused to find that someone had thought their lives worth dramatising. A survivor of the Mount Street Bridge Siege during the 1916 Rising saw my factual recreation of it for television and remarked: "Ah, it wasn't nearly as exciting as that!"

*Hugh Leonard.*

The Theatre Club would like to thank Hugh Leonard for his kindness in writing the programme note specially for this production.

Hugh Leonard will be remembered as the author of *Stephen D* presented by the Theatre Club in December 1971 and since *The Poker Session* (1963) he has written among other plays, *Mich and Mick* and *The Patrick Pearse Motel*. Well

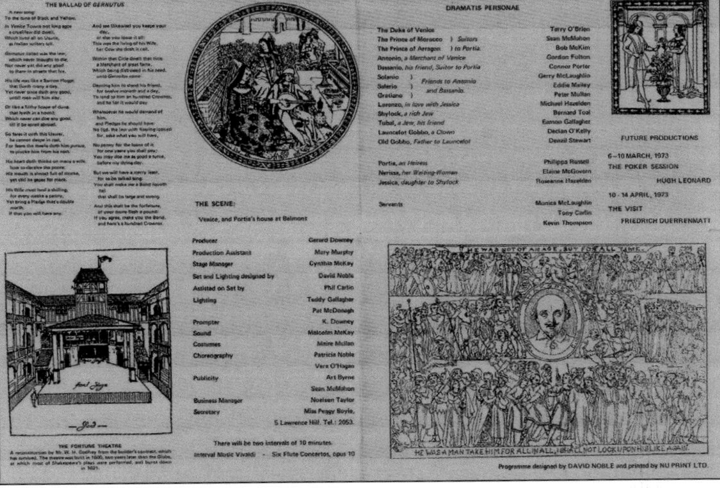

THE BALLAD OF *GERNUTUS*

DRAMATIS PERSONAE

| | |
|---|---|
| The Duke of Venice | Terry O'Brien |
| The Prince of Morocco ) *Suitors* | Sean McMahon |
| The Prince of Arragon ) *to Portia.* | Bob McKim |
| Antonio, *a Merchant of Venice* | Gordon Fulton |
| Bassanio, *his friend, Suitor to Portia* | Connor Porter |
| Solanio ) *Friends to Antonio* | Gerry McLaughlin |
| Salerio ) *and Bassanio.* | Eddie Mailey |
| Gratiano ) | Peter Mullan |
| Lorenzo, *in love with Jessica* | Michael Hazelden |
| Shylock, *a rich Jew* | Bernard Toal |
| Tubal, *a Jew, his friend* | Eamon Gallagher |
| Launcelot Gobbo, *a Clown* | Declan O'Kelly |
| Old Gobbo, *Father to Launcelot* | Denzil Stewart |
| Portia, *an Heiress* | Philippa Russell |
| Nerissa, *her Waiting-Woman* | Elaine McGovern |
| Jessica, *daughter to Shylock* | Roseanne Hazelden |
| Servants | Monica McLaughlin<br>Tony Carlin<br>Kevin Thompson |

THE SCENE:

Venice, and Portia's house at Belmont

| | |
|---|---|
| Producer | Gerard Downey |
| Production Assistant | Mary Murphy |
| Stage Manager | Cynthia McKay |
| Set and Lighting designed by | David Noble |
| Assisted on Set by | Phil Carlin |
| Lighting | Teddy Gallagher<br>Pat McDonagh |
| Prompter | K. Downey |
| Sound | Malcolm McKay |
| Costumes | Maire Mullan |
| Choreography | Patricia Noble<br>Vera O'Hagan |
| Publicity | Art Byrne<br>Sean McMahon |
| Business Manager | Noeleen Taylor |
| Secretary | Miss Peggy Boyle,<br>5 Lawrence Hill, Tel.: 2053. |

There will be two intervals of 10 minutes.

Interval Music Vivaldi - Six Flute Concertos, opus 10

THE FORTUNE THEATRE

FUTURE PRODUCTIONS

6–10 MARCH, 1973
THE POKER SESSION
HUGH LEONARD

10 - 14 APRIL, 1973
THE VISIT
FRIEDRICH DUERRENMATT

HE WAS NOT OF AN AGE, BUT FOR ALL TIME.

HE WAS A MAN TAKE HIM FOR ALL IN ALL, I SHALL NOT LOOK UPON HIS LIKE AGAIN.

Programme designed by DAVID NOBLE and printed by NU PRINT LTD.

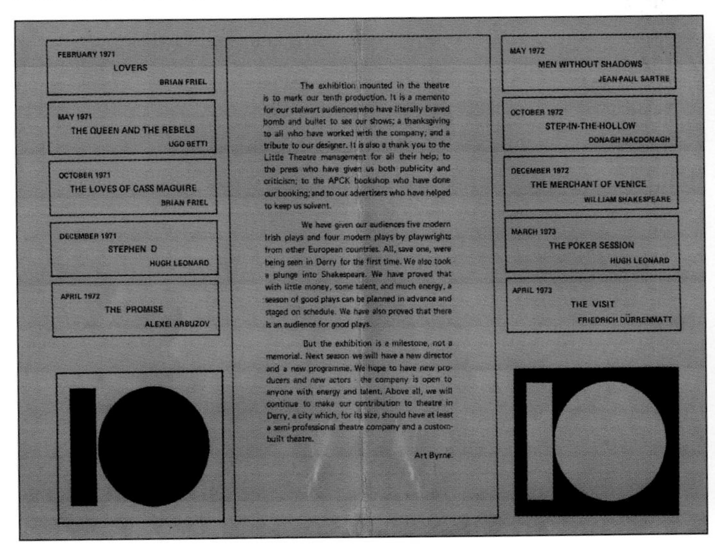

FEBRUARY 1971
LOVERS
BRIAN FRIEL

MAY 1971
THE QUEEN AND THE REBELS
UGO BETTI

OCTOBER 1971
THE LOVES OF CASS MAGUIRE
BRIAN FRIEL

DECEMBER 1971
STEPHEN D
HUGH LEONARD

APRIL 1972
THE PROMISE
ALEXEI ARBUZOV

The exhibition mounted in the theatre is to mark our tenth production. It is a memento for our stalwart audiences who have literally braved bomb and bullet to see our shows; a thanksgiving to all who have worked with the company; and a tribute to our designer. It is also a thank you to the Little Theatre management for all their help; to the press who have given us both publicity and criticism; to the APCK bookshop who have done our booking; and to our advertisers who have helped to keep us solvent.

We have given our audiences five modern Irish plays and four modern plays by playwrights from other European countries. All, save one, were being seen in Derry for the first time. We also took a plunge into Shakespeare. We have proved that with little money, some talent, and much energy, a season of good plays can be planned in advance and staged on schedule. We have also proved that there is an audience for good plays.

But the exhibition is a milestone, not a memorial. Next season we will have a new director and a new programme. We hope to have new producers and new actors - the company is open to anyone with energy and talent. Above all, we will continue to make our contribution to theatre in Derry, a city which, for its size, should have at least a semi-professional theatre company and a custom-built theatre.

Art Byrne.

MAY 1972
MEN WITHOUT SHADOWS
JEAN-PAUL SARTRE

OCTOBER 1972
STEP-IN-THE-HOLLOW
DONAGH MACDONAGH

DECEMBER 1972
THE MERCHANT OF VENICE
WILLIAM SHAKESPEARE

MARCH 1973
THE POKER SESSION
HUGH LEONARD

APRIL 1973
THE VISIT
FRIEDRICH DÜRRENMATT

Mr. Bernard Toal (director) rehearsing a scene with the principal members of the Theatre Club's cast of "Step in the Hollow" by Donagh Macdonagh, which opened last night in

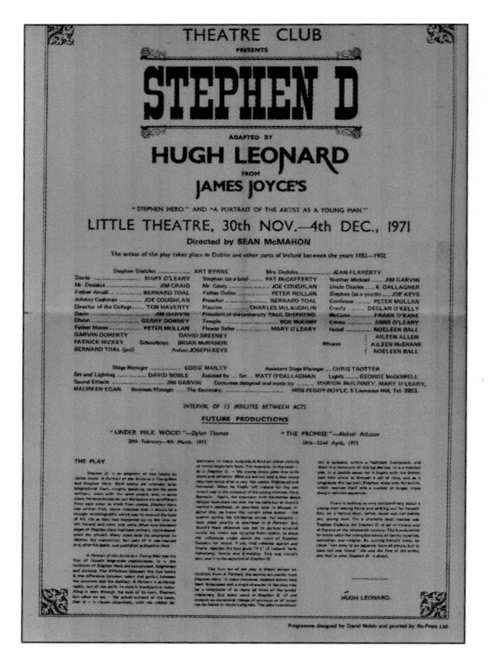
THEATRE CLUB
PRESENTS
STEPHEN D
ADAPTED BY
HUGH LEONARD
FROM
JAMES JOYCE'S
"STEPHEN HERO" AND "A PORTRAIT OF THE ARTIST AS A YOUNG MAN"
LITTLE THEATRE, 30th NOV.—4th DEC., 1971
Directed by SEAN McMAHON
The action of the play takes place in Dublin and other parts of Ireland between the years 1882—1902

Stephen Dedalus ........ ART BYRNE
Mrs. Dedalus ........ JEAN FLAHERTY
Dante ........ MARY O'LEARY
Mr. Dedalus ........ JIM CRAIG
Father Arnall ........ BERNARD TOAL
Johnny Cashman ........ JOE COUGHLAN
Director of the College ........ TOM HAVERTY
Davin ........ JIM GARVIN
Dixon ........ GERRY DOWNEY
Father Moran ........ PETER MULLAN
Stephen (as a boy) ........ PAT McCAFFERTY
Mr. Casey ........ JOE COUGHLAN
Father Dolan ........ PETER MULLAN
Preacher ........ BERNARD TOAL
Maurice ........ CHARLES McLAUGHLIN
President of the University ........ PAUL SHEPHERD
Temple ........ BOB McKIMM
Flower Seller ........ MARY O'LEARY
Brother Michael ........ JIM GARVIN
Uncle Charles ........ E. GALLAGHER
Stephen (as a youth) ........ JOE KEYS
Confessor ........ PETER MULLAN
Cranly ........ DECLAN O'KELLY
McCann ........ FRANK O'KANE
Emma ........ ANNE O'LEARY
Isobel ........ NOELEEN BALL
Schoolboys: GARVIN DOHERTY, PATRICK HICKEY, BERNARD TOAL (jun), DAVID SWEENEY, BRIAN McMAHON
Prefect: JOSEPH KEYS
Whores: AILEEN ALLEN, AILEEN McSHANE, NOELEEN BALL

Stage Manager ........ EDDIE MAILEY
Assistant Stage Manager ........ CHRIS TROTTER
Set and Lighting ........ DAVID NOBLE
Assisted by ........ MATT O'CALLAGHAN
Lights ........ GEORGE McDOWELL
Sound Effects ........ JIM GARVIN
Costumes designed and made by ........ MARION McILPINEY, MARY O'LEARY, MAUREEN EGAN
Business Manager ........ The Secretary, ........ MISS PEGGY BOYLE, 5 Lawrence Hill, Tel. 2053.

INTERVAL OF 15 MINUTES BETWEEN ACTS

FUTURE PRODUCTIONS

"UNDER MILK WOOD"—Dylan Thomas
29th February—4th March, 1972

"THE PROMISE"—Aleksei Arbuzov
18th—22nd April, 1972

THE PLAY

HUGH LEONARD

The cast of Ugo Betti's The Queen and the Rebels, the club's first play at the Little Theatre, as pictured in the Derry Journal in May 71. Includes a tooled-up Seán McMahon and a mac-wearing Art Byrne. Eddie Mailey, Gerry McLaughlin, Jean Flaherty, a rifle-carrying Peter Mullan and Gerry Downey are along the back. Aileen McShane, Paul Shepherd, Roy Seddon, Lawrence Overend, Mary Murphy and Ann O'Leary on the front row.

The Theatre Club's production of Brian Friel's The Loves of Cass McGuire, October 71. Includes: Mary O'Leary, Eddie Mailey, Mary Murphy, Ann O'Leary, Terry Willman, Gerry Rainey, Kevin McLaughlin, Jean Flaherty, Philippa Russell, Gerry Downey and producer Barney Toal.

The club's production of Brian Friel's Living Quarters in December 1979, featuring a cast of: Paul Wilkins, Pat Ferry, Connor Porter, Brenda Coyle, Mary Murphy, Eddie Mailey, Gerry Downey and Marilyn McLaughlin.

**Rivalries between local drama groups are more rumour than fact, and members of the Theatre Club (Barney Toal in this case) frequently partner with other groups for concerts, shows and pageants**

THE THEATRE CLUB PROUDLY PRESENT

VARIETY THEATRE

1. Mrs. Una O'Somachain
2. Mr. Jack Gallagher
3. Master Austin O'Donnell
4. Les Girls
5. Mr. David Noble
6. Mrs. Mary Murphy
7. AND MOST OF ALL YOURSELVES ........

(i) DAISY BELL – *Sung by Katie Lawrence.*
Daisy, Daisy - give me your answer do.
I'm half crazy - all for the love of you.
It won't be a stylish marriage,
I can't afford a carriage.
But you'll look sweet - upon the seat -
Of a bicycle built for two.

(ii) O - O - ANTONIO – *Sung by Florrie Forde.*
O - O - Antonio
He's gone away.
Left me alone-io
All on my own-io.
I'd like to meet him with his new sweetheart
Then up would go Antonio
– And his ice-cream cart.

(iii) ALL THE NICE GIRLS LOVE A SAILOR
*Sung by Hetty King.*
All the nice girls love a sailor.
All the nice girls love a tar.
For there's something about a sailor –
When you know waht sailors are.
Bright and breezy - free and easy
They're the ladies pride and joy.
Though they flirt with Kate and Jane –
Then it's off to sea again,
Ship Ahoy! Ship Ahoy!

(iv) AFTER THE BALL – *Sung by Chas. K. Harris.*
After the ball is over,
After the break of morn,
After the dancers leaving,
After the stars are gone.
Many a heart is aching
If you could read them all;
Many the hopes that have vanished,
After the ball.

(v) DOWN AT THE OLD BULL AND BUSH
*Sung by Florrie Forde.*
Come, come, come and make eyes at me
Down at the Old Bull and Bush - Tarararara.
Come, come, drink some port-wine with me,
Down at the Old Bull and Bush.
See the little German band - oompah, oompah, oompah.
Come, let me hold your hand, dear.
Come, come, come and have a drink with me,
Down at the Old Bull and Bush.

*INTERVAL OF 10 MINUTES*

MARIA MARTEN OR The MURDER IN THE RED BARN
Directed by GERRY DOWNEY.

## Theatre Club Presenting Friel Play

Next week Derry City play-goers will have the pleasure of seeing again one of the most popular of all Brian Friel's plays, "Philadelphia Here I Come," a play which is arguably the best in post-war Irish drama.

Those who have seen the play before will need no encouragement to come and see it again but for new play-goers it can be said that the play is a fine and rare tempering of humour and pathos to a very Irish and at the same time universal situation.

Gareth O'Donnell, son of a Donegal small shopkeeper, is leaving home at twenty-five years of age. But his cannot be a wholehearted emigration. As we watch the events and flashbacks of his last night at home, we realise that for him there are things which he cannot leave behind mentally. They will pain him all his life. His grief for his lost girl, his love for his father which remains agonisingly unspoken, his nostalgia for his boyhood, all are painted with humour and marvellous sympathy.

A striking stage device is used to portray the conflicts within Gar, the tugs to and fro, should he go, could he stay, what he thinks, what he feels, what he actually says. Two actors play Gar, both simultaneously present on the stage. One is his public face, the person as other people see him. The other is the private man, who voices the inner thoughts and longings that the public Gar cannot. Inner tensions are made actual and present, as it were, incarnated on stage.

The play was first produced in September 1964 at the Dublin Theatre Festival. It was an instant success and subsequently had a long run on Broadway. Both public and critics acclaimed it. Peter Lennon wrote in "The Guardian": "Mr. Friel examines with great delicacy and humour the circumstances and the kind of climate which made it inevitable that an Irish youth must emigrate . . . he has produced the unmistakable sound of real people talking to each other and in this case living through an important moment in their lives."

Next week's production will be by the Theatre Club directed by Gordon Fulton. It will play nightly at 8 p.m. in the Little Theatre from Monday to Saturday, 15th-20th December. Booking daily 2-5 p.m. at the Little Theatre, Orchard Street. Telephone 2880.

In our picture taken at rehearsal are, from left, Michael Gillen, who plays "Canon Byrne"; Jean Flaherty ("Madge"); Barney Toal ("S. B. O'Donnell"); Conor Porter ("the private Gar"); and Gerry Downey ("the public Gar").

**Gerry and Connor Porter play the two sides of Gar, in Gordon Fulton's production of the Brian Friel classic Philadelphia, Here I Come.**

**A press photocall for the principals in Stephen D: Jean Flaherty, Art Byrne and Jim Craig.**

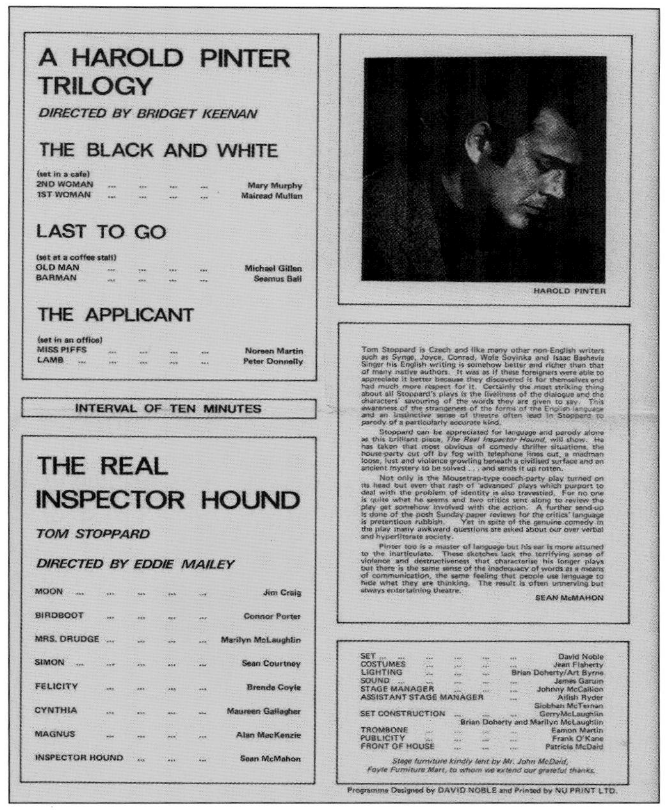

A HAROLD PINTER TRILOGY

*DIRECTED BY BRIDGET KEENAN*

THE BLACK AND WHITE

(set in a cafe)

| | |
|---|---|
| 2ND WOMAN ... ... ... ... | Mary Murphy |
| 1ST WOMAN ... ... ... ... | Mairead Mullan |

LAST TO GO

(set at a coffee stall)

| | |
|---|---|
| OLD MAN ... ... ... ... | Michael Gillen |
| BARMAN ... ... ... ... | Seamus Ball |

THE APPLICANT

(set in an office)

| | |
|---|---|
| MISS PIFFS ... ... ... ... | Noreen Martin |
| LAMB ... ... ... ... ... | Peter Donnelly |

INTERVAL OF TEN MINUTES

THE REAL INSPECTOR HOUND

*TOM STOPPARD*

*DIRECTED BY EDDIE MAILEY*

| | |
|---|---|
| MOON ... ... ... ... ... | Jim Craig |
| BIRDBOOT ... ... ... ... | Connor Porter |
| MRS. DRUDGE ... ... ... | Marilyn McLaughlin |
| SIMON ... ... ... ... ... | Sean Courtney |
| FELICITY ... ... ... ... | Brenda Coyle |
| CYNTHIA ... ... ... ... | Maureen Gallagher |
| MAGNUS ... ... ... ... | Alan MacKenzie |
| INSPECTOR HOUND ... ... ... | Sean McMahon |

HAROLD PINTER

Tom Stoppard is Czech and like many other non-English writers such as Synge, Joyce, Conrad, Wole Soyinka and Isaac Bashevis Singer his English writing is somehow better and richer than that of many native authors. It was as if these foreigners were able to appreciate it better because they discovered it for themselves and had much more respect for it. Certainly the most striking thing about all Stoppard's plays is the liveliness of the dialogue and the characters' savouring of the words they are given to say. This awareness of the strangeness of the forms of the English language and an instinctive sense of theatre often lead in Stoppard to parody of a particularly accurate kind.

Stoppard can be appreciated for language and parody alone as this brilliant piece, *The Real Inspector Hound*, will show. He has taken that most obvious of comedy thriller situations, the house-party cut off by fog with telephone lines cut, a madman loose, lust and violence growling beneath a civilised surface and an ancient mystery to be solved . . . and sends it up rotten.

Not only is the Mousetrap-type coach-party play turned on its head but even that rash of 'advanced' plays which purport to deal with the problem of identity is also travestied. For no one is quite what he seems and two critics sent along to review the play get somehow involved with the action. A further send-up is done of the posh Sunday-paper reviews for the critics' language is pretentious rubbish. Yet in spite of the genuine comedy in the play many awkward questions are asked about our over verbal and hyperliterate society.

Pinter too is a master of language but his ear is more attuned to the inarticulate. These sketches lack the terrifying sense of violence and destructiveness that characterise his longer plays but there is the same sense of the inadequacy of words as a means of communication, the same feeling that people use language to hide what they are thinking. The result is often unnerving but always entertaining theatre.

SEAN McMAHON

| | |
|---|---|
| SET ... ... ... ... ... ... | David Noble |
| COSTUMES ... ... ... ... | Jean Flaherty |
| LIGHTING ... ... ... | Brian Doherty/Art Byrne |
| SOUND ... ... ... ... ... | James Garuin |
| STAGE MANAGER ... ... ... | Johnny McCallion |
| ASSISTANT STAGE MANAGER ... | Ailish Ryder |
| | Siobhan McTernan |
| SET CONSTRUCTION ... ... ... | GerryMcLaughlin |
| | Brian Doherty and Marilyn McLaughlin |
| TROMBONE ... ... ... ... | Eamon Martin |
| PUBLICITY ... ... ... ... | Frank O'Kane |
| FRONT OF HOUSE ... ... ... | Patricia McDaid |

*Stage furniture kindly lent by Mr. John McDaid, Foyle Furniture Mart, to whom we extend our grateful thanks.*

Programme Designed by DAVID NOBLE and Printed by NU PRINT LTD.

**An early lead role for Monica McLaughlin (later Monica Garvin), pictured here holding a bottle, with Gerry Downey and Mickey Gillen in the 1974 production of The Fire Raisers. Monica and her husband Jim would be one of (at least) three couples who would meet through the Theatre Club, others being Ann and Jim Craig, and Marilyn and Gerry McLaughlin.**

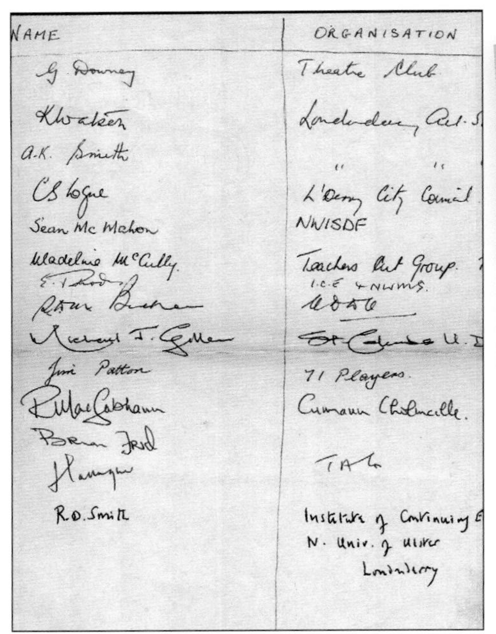

| NAME | ORGANISATION |
| --- | --- |
| G. Downey | Theatre Club |
| [illegible] | Londonderry Cul. S |
| A.K. Smith | " " |
| CS Logue | L'Derry City Council |
| Sean Mc Mahon | NWISDF |
| Madeline McCully | Teachers Art Group |
| E. Rhodes | I.C.E + NWMS |
| [illegible] | [illegible] |
| Michael J. Gillen | [illegible] |
| Jim Patton | 71 Players |
| [illegible] | [illegible] |
| Brian Friel | |
| [illegible] | TAG |
| R.O. Smith | Institute of Continuing E N. Univ. of Ulster Londonderry |

A Theatre Action Group sign-in sheet from May 1974, featuring, amongst others, Brian Friel and the former BBC producer Reggie Smith (who is alleged by MI5 to be a communist spy).

When TAG winds up, Cormac Downey inherits all the group's charred stationery, which in turn sees him develop a sideline as a book illustrator and cartoonist.

# INTERMISSION I: THE THEATRE ACTION GROUP

The lack of a proper theatre venue in Derry became more pronounced in the 1970s, with the bombing of the Guildhall and its long-term closure. There was nowhere left to host national or international repertory companies, even if they had wished to come.

Gerry, along with fellow teachers and theatre-lovers, Mickey Gillen and Rusty Gallagher put together a purposeful campaign team, the Theatre Action Group (TAG), to lobby for a new, purpose-built facility for the city.

Playwright Brian Friel was an early and active committee member, stressing the need also for a professional theatre company to accompany any new building.

Two influential lecturers from the Institute of Continuing Education (ICE) at Magee, Professors Ted Rhodes and Reggie Smith, also joined – as they were keen for the theatre to be used by their staff and students.

Most of the region's drama and music groups, along with Derry Council, were represented on the new committee, as were the opera-loving editor of the Londonderry Sentinel, Sidney Buchanan, and the high-profile novelist, Jennifer Johnston. Architect Tom Mullarkey was also recruited to the campaign, producing a model for the new theatre, which was displayed in the council offices. (Mullarkey would later design the Ardhowen Theatre in Enniskillen.)

The committee set about raising money for the campaign, with Niall Toibin and Phil Coulter volunteering their services for fundraisers.

In one aside, the committee purchased a large stock of branded stationery, which was stored in a press at Gerry's home in Crawford Square. Unfortunately, a child who had recently been forced to sit through the Theatre Club's production of The Fire Raisers, inadvertently set the said press alight, and all the surviving stationery ended up with scorch marks. Mickey Gillen, however, was way ahead of his time, and instructed Gerry to continue to keep the materials for correspondence as they would perfectly convey the image of war-torn Derry in need of artistic intervention to save the city.

Ultimately, after years of being strung along by Direct Rule ministers who could see no benefit to them of opening a theatre in Derry, TAG dissolved and they had to wait until 2001 until the Millennium Forum was built.

After the group broke up, young Cormac Downey got to keep thousands of charred TAG envelopes which he carefully opened out to draw on and kick start his hobby as a cartoonist. Every cloud, and all that. Gerry was TAG's first Company Secretary, and kept meticulous hand-written minutes of the meetings, which provide a great insight into both the campaign and Derry society at that time. Indeed, they are worth another book in their own right.

**Marilyn McLaughlin moves from leading lady to director for this November 1980 production of The Importance of Being Earnest.**

*Shakespeare*

**THE TEMPEST**

BRITANNIA HALL
20 - 22 February 1992

**The 1980s see members of the Theatre Club start to branch off in different directions, many gaining professional stripes. In 1986, several TC regulars, including Mairead Mullan and Jean Flaherty, are involved in the film The Best Man which wins a Celtic Film Festival award.**

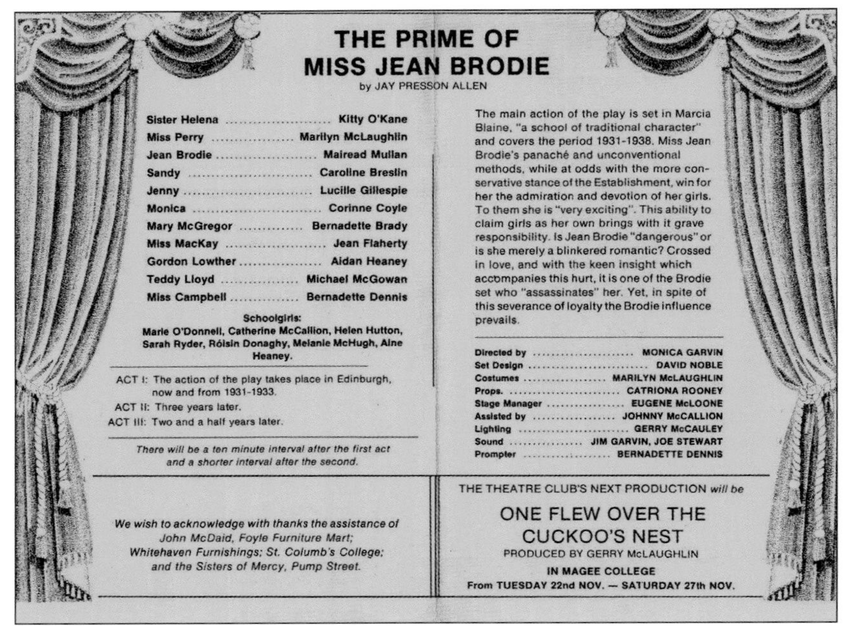

**THE PRIME OF MISS JEAN BRODIE**
by JAY PRESSON ALLEN

| | |
|---|---|
| Sister Helena | Kitty O'Kane |
| Miss Perry | Marilyn McLaughlin |
| Jean Brodie | Mairead Mullan |
| Sandy | Caroline Breslin |
| Jenny | Lucille Gillespie |
| Monica | Corinne Coyle |
| Mary McGregor | Bernadette Brady |
| Miss MacKay | Jean Flaherty |
| Gordon Lowther | Aidan Heaney |
| Teddy Lloyd | Michael McGowan |
| Miss Campbell | Bernadette Dennis |

**Schoolgirls:**
Marie O'Donnell, Catherine McCallion, Helen Hutton, Sarah Ryder, Róisín Donaghy, Melanie McHugh, Aine Heaney.

ACT I: The action of the play takes place in Edinburgh, now and from 1931-1933.
ACT II: Three years later.
ACT III: Two and a half years later.

*There will be a ten minute interval after the first act and a shorter interval after the second.*

*We wish to acknowledge with thanks the assistance of John McDaid, Foyle Furniture Mart; Whitehaven Furnishings; St. Columb's College; and the Sisters of Mercy, Pump Street.*

The main action of the play is set in Marcia Blaine, "a school of traditional character" and covers the period 1931-1938. Miss Jean Brodie's panaché and unconventional methods, while at odds with the more conservative stance of the Establishment, win for her the admiration and devotion of her girls. To them she is "very exciting". This ability to claim girls as her own brings with it grave responsibility. Is Jean Brodie "dangerous" or is she merely a blinkered romantic? Crossed in love, and with the keen insight which accompanies this hurt, it is one of the Brodie set who "assassinates" her. Yet, in spite of this severance of loyalty the Brodie influence prevails.

| | |
|---|---|
| Directed by | MONICA GARVIN |
| Set Design | DAVID NOBLE |
| Costumes | MARILYN McLAUGHLIN |
| Props. | CATRIONA ROONEY |
| Stage Manager | EUGENE McLOONE |
| Assisted by | JOHNNY McCALLION |
| Lighting | GERRY McCAULEY |
| Sound | JIM GARVIN, JOE STEWART |
| Prompter | BERNADETTE DENNIS |

THE THEATRE CLUB'S NEXT PRODUCTION *will be*
ONE FLEW OVER THE CUCKOO'S NEST
PRODUCED BY GERRY McLAUGHLIN
IN MAGEE COLLEGE
From TUESDAY 22nd NOV. — SATURDAY 27th NOV.

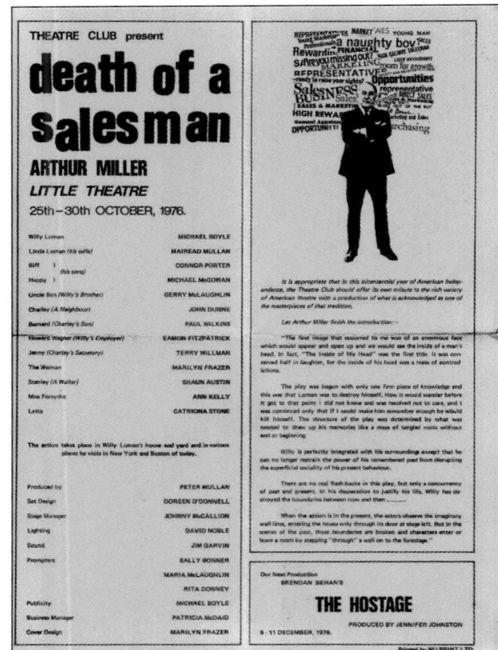

THEATRE CLUB present

**death of a salesman**

**ARTHUR MILLER**
*LITTLE THEATRE*
25th–30th OCTOBER, 1976.

| | |
|---|---|
| Willy Loman | MICHAEL BOYLE |
| Linda Loman *(his wife)* | MAIREAD MULLAN |
| Biff *(his sons)* | CONNOR PORTER |
| Happy *(his sons)* | MICHAEL McGOWAN |
| Uncle Ben *(Willy's Brother)* | GERRY McLAUGHLIN |
| Charley *(A Neighbour)* | JOHN DUNNE |
| Bernard *(Charley's Son)* | PAUL WILKINS |
| Howard Wagner *(Willy's Employer)* | EAMON FITZPATRICK |
| Jenny *(Charley's Secretary)* | TERRY WILLMAN |
| The Woman | MARILYN FRAZER |
| Stanley *(A Waiter)* | SHAUN AUSTIN |
| Miss Forsythe | ANN KELLY |
| Letta | CATRIONA STONE |

The action takes place in Willy Loman's house and yard and in various places he visits in New York and Boston of today.

| | |
|---|---|
| Produced by | PETER MULLAN |
| Set Design | DOREEN O'DONNELL |
| Stage Manager | JOHNNY McCALLION |
| Lighting | DAVID NOBLE |
| Sound | JIM GARVIN |
| Prompters | SALLY BONNER |
| | MARIA McLAUGHLIN |
| | RITA DOWNEY |
| Publicity | MICHAEL BOYLE |
| Business Manager | PATRICIA McDAID |
| Cover Design | MARILYN FRAZER |



*It is appropriate that in this bicentennial year of American Independence, the Theatre Club should offer its own tribute to the rich variety of American theatre with a production of what is acknowledged as one of the masterpieces of that tradition.*

*Let Arthur Miller finish the introduction:—*

"The first image that occurred to me was of an enormous face which would appear and open up and we would see the inside of a man's head. In fact, "The Inside of His Head" was the first title. It was conceived half in laughter, for the inside of his head was a mass of contradictions.

The play was begun with only one firm piece of knowledge and this was that Loman was to destroy himself. How it would wander before it got to that point I did not know and was resolved not to care, and I was convinced only that if I could make him remember enough he would kill himself. The structure of the play was determined by what was needed to draw up his memories like a mass of tangled roots without end or beginning.

Willy is perfectly integrated with his surroundings except that he can no longer restrain the power of his remembered past from disrupting the superficial sociality of his present behaviour.

There are no real flash-backs in this play, but only a concurrency of past and present. In his desperation to justify his life, Willy has destroyed the boundaries between now and then ..........

When the action is in the present, the actors observe the imaginary wall-lines, entering the house only through its door at stage left. But in the scenes of the past, those boundaries are broken and characters enter or leave a room by stepping "through" a wall on to the forestage."

Our Next Production
BRENDAN BEHAN'S
**THE HOSTAGE**
PRODUCED BY JENNIFER JOHNSTON
6 - 11 DECEMBER, 1976.

Printed by NU PRINT LTD.

**THEATRE CLUB** *presents ....*

# PLAZA SUITE

**A COMEDY BY NEIL SIMON**

**Great Hall Magee College N.U.U.**

**26th - 30th NOV. (incl.)**

**8.00 p.m. Nightly**

**ADMISSION £2.00 (£1.00 CONCESSIONARY)**

Booking Rialto Entertainment Centre, Tel. 260516

PRINTED BY FIVE LAMP PRINTERS LTD., LONDON STREET.

Members of the cast of the Theatre Club production of 'Plaza Suite' by Neil Simon, which ran at Magee College. At front are Catriona Stone and Jim Craig, with at back from left, Jean Flaherty, Marie O'Keeney, Denis McGowan, Marilyn McLaughlin and Bart O'Donnell. (0611MM03)

**Ann Craig directs husband Jim in Neil Simon's three-act comedy Plaza Suite at the Great Hall in Magee in November 1985.**

# ACT II
# THE 1970s: KEEPING THE CANDLE LIT

*(Interior: A little theatre, where performers play on a well-lit stage. Noises: a buzzing audience interrupted occasionally by sirens, gunfire and distant explosions.)*

The programme notes for Lovers, the Theatre Club's first staged play in 1971, set out a mission statement from which the club would never veer, even in the darkest times: everyone must be welcome to join the group, and everyone must be welcome to watch the performances.

To this end the club was calling for a new civic theatre for Derry, which 'would be neither "sanctified" nor forced to play an old Austrian tune; all citizens could frequent it with their principles intact'. Remember, this was a time when church officials hand-selected the theatre schedules in some parts, while the British national anthem was played in others.

As one member succinctly put it, in a time of increasing social segregation the Theatre Club was completely non-sectarian – or 'co-ed', to use the preferred teachers' vernacular. It was a place to celebrate art and cement friendships; an escape from the politics of the outside world.

For much of the decade, the Theatre Club and the 71 Players (which also operated from the Little Theatre) were the only arts societies in the entire region keeping the candle lit. But it wasn't always easy. Performances were interrupted or occasionally cancelled because of bomb alerts on the neighbouring Foyle Street. Players and audiences often had to negotiate riots, British army checkpoints and, in some cases, republican and loyalist barricades to get to shows or rehearsals.

(There is a famous story about how when the comedian Frank Carson was emceeing a variety night at St Columb's Hall in the late 1960s, he appeared after the interval and announced that someone had just thrown a petrol bomb into a nearby hostelry. The audience gasped, only to be told: "But it's okay, one of the regulars drank it...")

The Theatre Club carried out its selection of plays with great care and respect to would-be audiences. Unsurprisingly, the schedule included anti-war pieces such as Shadow of a Gunman and The Hostage; dramas railing against the death penalty such as The Quare Fella; and plays challenging outdated mores and highlighting social hypocrisy, from the pen of Brian Friel and others. On occasions when things were very black outside, the club sometimes responded with comedies, farce and romance.

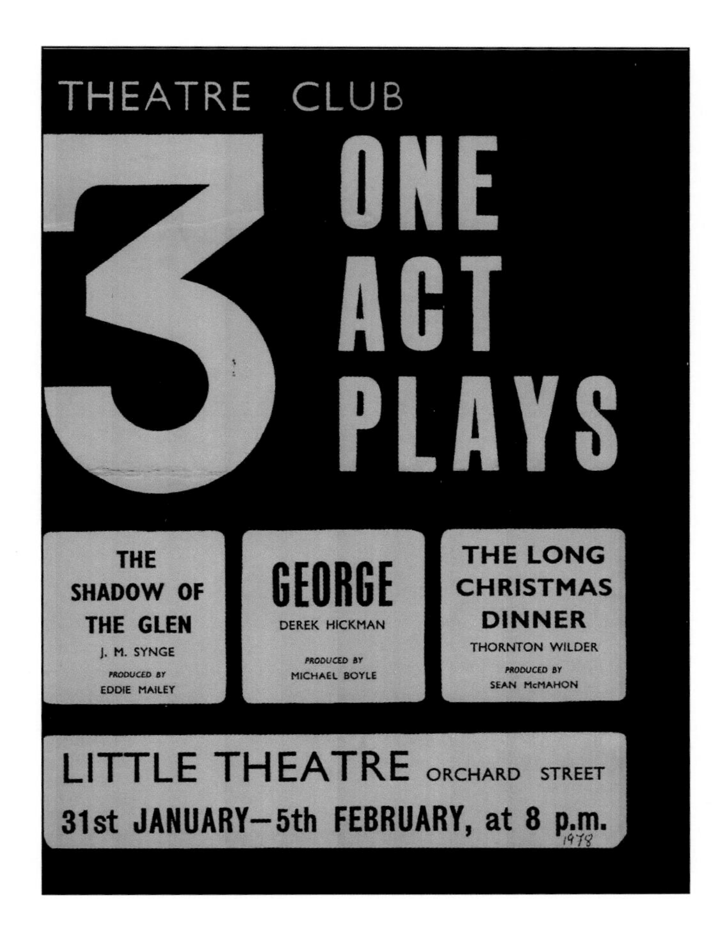

**Most of the club's players also teach, coach or judge school drama. Emerging players in programme for the 72 City of Derry Inter-Schools Drama Festival include: the future Press Ombudsman Susan McKay, Bart O'Donnell and Joe Keys who became TC mainstays, the barrister and university lecturer John Thompson, and Jimmy Cadden who became editor of the Londonderry Sentinel. Amanda Burton, later of BBC's Silent Witness, is another product of the Londonderry High School (LHS) Drama Club of this era, and is loaned out to the (all-boys) St Columb's DS for musicals.**

The choices didn't always work out and during at least one European play, the numbers on the stage are said to have outnumbered those in the stalls. Comedies and Shakespearean plays (which were a staple on the Northern Ireland exam syllabus) generally attracted decent crowds. This was important, as the Theatre Club received no grants or sponsorship, and had to break even. Club members who weren't in the cast would pay to watch performances to support the kitty - and they would also do the same for their supposed rivals in the '71 Players, who faced identical strictures. (Editor's note: the players also paid the admission fees for their families, but while Gerry loved to bring his children to the plays, he was always careful to ensure the content was suitable for sensitive minds. After he barred Garbhán from attending The Hostage – in which Gerry was playing the rent boy Rio Rita, his ten-year-old son hunted down and devoured a copy of the script, and has been a Behan fan ever since.)

Finding space for rehearsals and auditions could be problematic as the Little Theatre was rarely available, other than for performance. But the sense of purpose and determination that pervaded the company ensured that all obstacles must be overcome. The McMahons had a big house and practice sessions could take place in the attic or, if numbers were smaller, in the warmer kitchen. Indeed, back in 1971, when a young Jim Craig went for his first Theatre Club try-out in that same kitchen, he found himself sharing the rail of the Aga with a young actress called Ann O'Leary. Derryman Jim was very taken with Ann's southern brogue, and they are now married almost 50 years.

Props were borrowed from friends and family, while wardrobe mistress Anita Robinson would perform miracles with costumes. David Noble, an art teacher at Londonderry High School, was a genius at set design and producing posters and programmes. Ted Gallagher, a professional photographer, was a dab hand at getting the lighting perfect. As a backstage team, they were unbeatable.

Freelance wardrobe designing was discouraged after one actor's lovestruck fiancée fashioned him a far more glorious Shakespearean costume than any of the other (lead) players were wearing. "It was so awful, so overdone," she confessed many years later. "He was so glamorous and everyone else looked like a poor man's Robin Hood."

Sets, as any player will tell you, didn't always serve their purpose. During the club's staging of Hamlet, a curtain (arras), supposed to conceal Polonius who is spying on the Prince, was accidentally dislodged by Connor Porter's swinging sword, revealing Barney Toal smoking happily on his pipe as he waited for his cue.

The same play also saw sound engineer Jim Garvin make mischief in the closing scenes, where nine of the cast were laying supposedly dead on the Little Theatre stage. Garvin would change the sombre music for the ending each night until the final performance, when he decided to play the Overture from William Tell. All the corpses, of course, shook with laughter. ("We wanted to kill him," said one.)

As the company's reputation grew, so too did the size of the troupe – and its ambition. In 1972, Gerry, who was producing Merchant of Venice, recruited the recently-returned student Connor Porter, who had acted at both St Columb's and Queen's.

Porter had played the lead in the St Columb's DS version of Hamlet and would later reprise the role for the Theatre Club, as directed by another gifted draftee, the former BBC producer Reggie Smith. Hamlet is too long a play for a full performance and most directors would cut the script pre-rehearsal. But Smith would pull out a stopwatch during rehearsals to time scenes, which he then cut as they went along, thus testing young Porter's excellent memory no end.

New arrivals Marilyn McLaughlin (née Frazer) and Mairead Mullan were also both consummate performers, while Monica Garvin and her husband Jim would become the cornerstones of the production team. Mullan, who had previously won national awards with the Gaelic League Drama Society in Dungannon and had performed with the Circle Drama Club in Belfast while training as a teacher, made her Theatre Club debut as the lead in Juno in the Paycock in 1974. After many stage productions, she would go on to star in the film The Best Man in 1986 and work with Joe Mahon on numerous Irish-language TV productions, as both a narrator and costume designer. She actually met her husband Peter, on stage. (See Dramatis Personae for more.)

The Dublin-born novelist Jennifer Johnston, whose mother was a professional director and father was an actor, was another great catch for the club. She produced at least three plays during the 1970s, (Shadow of a Gunman, The Hostage and one of her own), and was also an advisor to the Theatre Action Group. She is remembered as 'very, very professional', and the players said they learned a lot from her.

Talk to some of the older hands today, and you will see faces light up as they remember the camaraderie that existed and the real fun that they had. If things were getting too heavy, it wasn't unheard of for a younger player to prank one of the seniors to lighten the mood – even mid-show. A corpse might wink at a grieving mother, or a player would change a cue at the last minute to test if the recipient was awake.

Jim Craig was said to be the most "impish" of the lot and would regularly tell jokes sotto voce during the most serious scenes to try and get his co-actors to crack. "It was a nightmare trying to keep a straight face," recalled one leading lady.

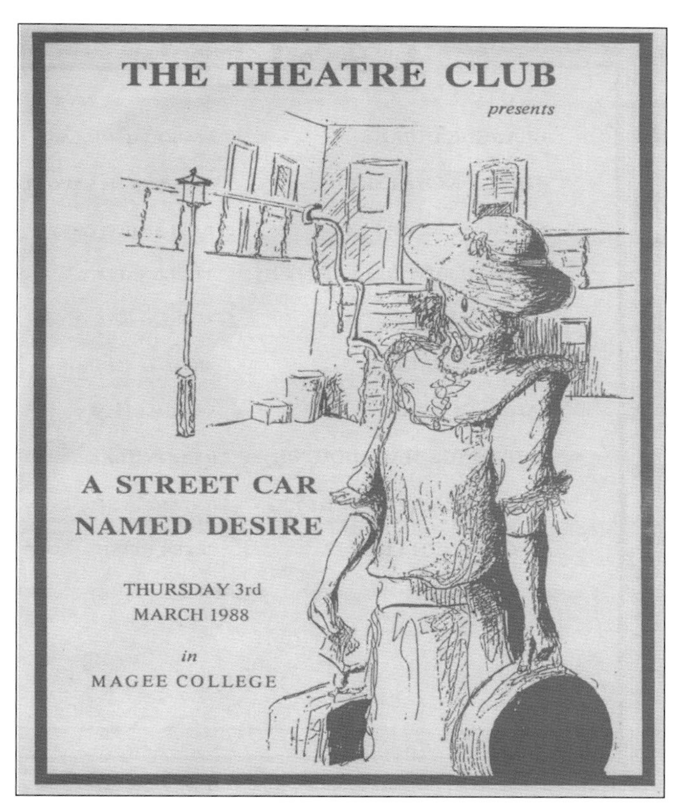


**Mairead Mullan, again, is mesmerising as Blanche in this TC production of the 1951 Tennesse Williams drama A Streetcar Named Desire. Directed by Gerry, the play is staged at Magee College.**

CAST

| | | | |
|---|---|---|---|
| BLANCHE DUBOIS | MAIREAD MULLAN | DIRECTED BY | GERARD DOWNEY |
| STELLA KEWALSKI | MARILYN Mc LAUGHLIN | DESIGN | BRIAN O' CONNOR |
| STANLEY KEWALSKI | PAUL O' DOH ERTY | STAGE MANAGER | CATHY MULLAN |
| HAROLD MITCHELL (MITCH) | TIM CONNELLY | LIGHTS | GERRY Mc CAULEY |
| EUNICE HUBBEL | MARIE O' KEENEY | SOUND | BILLY GALLAGHER |
| STEVE HUBBEL | BRIAN O' CONNOR | PROMPTER | AGNES Mc GUINNESS |
| PABLO GONZALES | SEAN MARTIN | FRONT OF HOUSE | PATRICIA Mc DAID |
| A STRANGE MAN (DOCTOR) | BARNEY TOAL | PUBLICITY | JIM CRAIG |
| A STRANGE WOMAN(NURSE) | CATRIONA STONE | | EDDIE MAILEY |
| A YOUNG COLLECTOR | PETER QUINN | POSTER AND PROGRAMME | UNA MAILEY |

Mostly, they got away with it. But Gerry recalls being contacted one evening by Seán McMahon who had just received a call from an irate Brian Friel. Apparently the publicist appointed by Gerry for their production of Friel's latest play – with the perennial instruction to put bums on seats – had got off the leash. The play, which had a couple of adult themes, was currently being described in the local press as 'dirtier than a weekend in Bundoran'.

Friel was understandably protective of his image as he had recently been targeted by British critics over Freedom of the City, which features British soldiers shooting Derry civilians in cold blood (as the playwright himself had witnessed on Bloody Sunday). The novitiate publicist was relieved of his responsibilities but, as was the way with the club, he was quickly forgiven and transferred to other duties.

Most of the troupe were famously inept when it came to 'modern' technology. And improvisation while the mother of invention could also be a parent of disaster. One actor playing the ghost of Hamlet's father was given a small torch to wear in an old-style helmet fashioned by wardrobe mistress Anita Armstrong. The idea was Ted Gallagher would dim the stage lights, and the ghost could walk across the stage lit up by his own steam. Ethereal, was the term used. On opening night when the lights went out, however, the player, who hadn't tested the kit, found himself blinded by the torch and walked into the proscenium with a terrible clatter. Not the most convincing look for a ghost.

Audiences were generally appreciative though - too appreciative at times. When the '71 Players produced a play in which the vivacious Noeleen Ball appeared on stage as a mummy wrapped in very tight bandages, the solicitor Claude Wilton let out a loud grunt of approval from the stalls that sent the audience into paroxysms.

Then there's the story of how the gentleman street drinker, 'Gackawacka', somehow wandered into the Little Theatre and down the aisle halfway through a very emotive exchange in the Playboy of the Western World. He began ad-libbing, throwing the players into considerable confusion and sending the audience into convulsions, before theatre caretaker Jimmy Larmour quietly led him away.

Not forgetting, of course, how raconteur Barney Toal would often reduce the company to fits of laughter with his shaggy dog stories – such as when a Foyle Street working girl propositioned him on his way to a show, asking him if he wanted 'a good time'. 'Daughter,' he told her, 'at my age if I want a good time, I'm going to need two weeks' notice...'

It really was the best of times in the worst of times.

Gerry McLaughlin produces this October 1975 production of Tarry Flynn, with Jim Craig in the lead role.

The caption has been cut off this clipping reviewing/previewing a Theatre Club play, which features Philippa Russell, Connor Porter, Jim Garvin, Eddie Mailey, Gordon Fulton and Gerry.

| | Credit | Debit |
|---|---|---|
| To Subscriptions from members | £ 54-50 | |
| "Step-in-the-Hollow" Expenditure | | £ 12-06½ |
| The Playboy of the Western World | | |
| Takings at door | 2-25 | |
| Expenditure | | 5-07½ |
| The Importance of being Earnest | | |
| Takings at door | 2-40 | |
| Expenditure | | 6-00 |
| Death & Resurrection of Mr. Roche | | |
| Takings at door | 2-70 | |
| Expenditure | | 10-26½ |
| The House of Bernarda Alba | | |
| Takings at door | 5-65 | |
| Expenditure | | 7-60 |
| Long Day's Journey into Night | | |
| Takings at door | 2-10 | |
| Expenditure | | 5-75 |
| Philadelphia, Here I come | | |
| Expenditure | | 3-25 |
| "Lovers" (Stage Production) | | |
| Box Office Takings | 159-00 | |
| Expenditure | | 127-36 |
| "The Queen & the Rebels" (Stage Production) | | |
| Box Office Takings & Sale of Programmes | 148-37 | |
| Expenditure | | 110-65 |
| To Hotel, A.G.M. Sept.,1970 | | 1-25 |
| Advertising for same | | 2-57½ |
| Stationery, phone calls, etc. | | 2-26 |
| Bank charges | | 1-08 |
| TOTAL | £ 376-97 | £ 295-18 |
| Balance | | £ 81-79 |
| | £ 376-97 | £ 376-97 |

OVER/

The Treasurer's Statement from 1970/71, which includes mention of seven rehearsed readings before the Theatre Company's debut stage production, Lovers. The club's reading of The Death & Resurrection of Mr Roche shows door receipts of £2.70 versus outgoings of £10.261/2.

# "THE BEST MAN" OFF TO DUBLIN

"The Best Man" the feature film made by the Northlands Centre, Derry, has been invited to form part of the major Irish Film Festival "Contempor Eire." The Festival takes place in Dublin from September 28 to October 11, 1984. "The Best Man" will be screened on the last night of the Festival—October 11, 1984. The producers of the film see this as a major breakthrough for the film and the opening of possibilities for other films to be made in the North-West.

"The Best Man," which received great acclaim after its premiere and public showing in Derry, deals with a weekend in the life of Billy Maguire, a happy-go-lucky Derryman and his preparations for the wedding of one of his friends. Billy is the sort of character only too familiar in public houses. He's the ageing bachelor with the chat and the crack who gaily drinks and gambles whilst holding forth to the assembled company. The film traces a weekend in Billy's life. It begins with Billy's recovery from another Friday night, going about his Saturday afternoon ritual of backing the horses and downing pints, leading to the stag night, and ends with a friend's wedding. Life is a romp with Billy at the head and he demands that his friends follow his tune.

Maureen and Jamsie, his married friends, interrupt Billy's world and ask questions of it. Challenging Billy's attitudes is the world of marriage, the world of children, responsibility, trust, love. They ask for a place but as Maureen re-discovers there is no place for them in Billy. He fears to be quiet, to hear himself. He cannot afford to go beyond his jokes. Maureen is Billy's only open challenger — the men need him too much to expose him and Jamsie lies somewhere in between.

"The Best Man" was filmed by Terence McDonald, a man who has gained a considerable reputation over the years as a documentary film-maker. It was scripted and directed by Joe Mahon and produced by Denis Bradley, Director of Northands Centre. The principal actors, Seamus Ball, Denis McGowan and Mairead Mullan, are well-known in amateur dramatic circles in Northern Ireland as are the other members of the strong supporting case: Mickey McGowan, Aiden Heaney and Jean Flaherty. The music in the film has received much acclaim. It was written and performed by Eamon Friel, whose music is well known to listeners of Radio Foyle and Radio Ulster.

Seamus Ball as Billy (left) and Denis McGowan as Jamsie in "The Best Man."

Seamus Ball and Denis McGowan enjoying success with The Best Man

THE THEATRE CLUB

— presents —

SUMMER

A Comedy By Hugh Leonard

WEDNESDAY, 2nd NOVEMBER 1988

until

SATURDAY, 5th NOVEMBER 1988

in

THE GREAT HALL, MAGEE COLLEGE

A first outing as director in November 1988 for Brian O'Connor, a successful architect who will later work for a time in professional theatre. Hugh Leonard's Summer, staged at Magee College, focuses on Ireland's get-rich-quick society, still a foreign concept to Derry audiences, who have never known the burden of wealth. There was also an appeal on the back of the programme for 'a dry garage' to store sets.

Best wishes to The Barber and his patrons

The Barber of Seville by Beaumarchais

| | |
|---|---|
| Count Almaviva, *a Spanish Grandee* | Brian O'Connor |
| Figaro, *a Barber of Seville* | Nevin Harris |
| Rosine, *a young lady of noble birth, ward of Bartholo* | Kitty O'Kane |
| Bartholo, *physician and Rosine's guardian* | Tim Connelly |
| Bazile, *music master to Rosine* | Jim Craig |
| Wakeful, *servant to Bartholo, a dull sleepy boy* | Ciaran McAlister |
| Youthful, *an elderly servant of Bartholo* | John Quigley |
| A Notary | Ciaran McAlister |
| An Alcalde | John Quigley |

| | | | |
|---|---|---|---|
| Director | Cora Baker (King) | Prompts | Lea Aylett |
| Set Design | Gavin Gallagher | Props | Marie O'Keeney |
| Lighting | Martin McDonald | | Cathy Mullan |
| Sound | Patrick Doherty | Stage Manager | Tracy Cullen |
| Costumes | *Changing Faces* | Publicity | Martin Bradley |
| Masks | Lawrence Price | | |

Scene: Seville, first outside Bartholo's house beneath Rosine's window, thereafter inside. The action takes place all on one day. The interval will be after act two.

Act one: afternoon — Act three: late evening
Act two: early evening — Act four: late at night

*We especially wish to acknowledge the help of Gerry Downey and the N-West College of Technology, St. Mary's Community Centre, and Fox's Corner for the loan of props.*

Cora Baker directs this 1993 Theatre Club production of The Barber of Seville

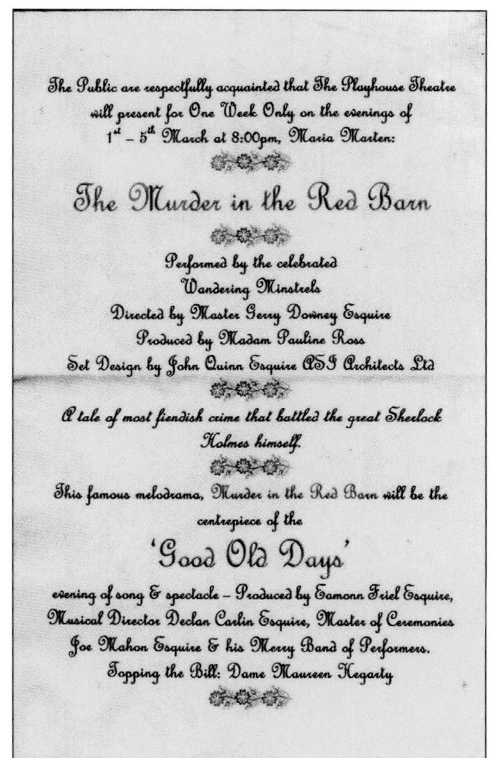

The Public are respectfully acquainted that The Playhouse Theatre will present for One Week Only on the evenings of 1st – 5th March at 8:00pm, Maria Marten:

The Murder in the Red Barn

Performed by the celebrated Wandering Minstrels

Directed by Master Gerry Downey Esquire

Produced by Madam Pauline Ross

Set Design by John Quinn Esquire ASJ Architects Ltd

A tale of most fiendish crime that baffled the great Sherlock Holmes himself.

This famous melodrama, Murder in the Red Barn will be the centrepiece of the

'Good Old Days'

evening of song & spectacle – Produced by Eamonn Friel Esquire, Musical Director Declan Carlin Esquire, Master of Ceremonies Joe Mahon Esquire & his Merry Band of Performers.

Topping the Bill: Dame Maureen Hegarty

The Theatre Club enjoys a second trip into the archives for this barnstorming production of Maria Marten: Murder in the Red Barn, at the Derry Playhouse. Gerry directs again, but this time Connor Porter takes the part of the evil villain Corder, and is never better. As before, the audience is treated to a Good Old Days variety concert, produced here by Eamon Friel and Declan Carlin.

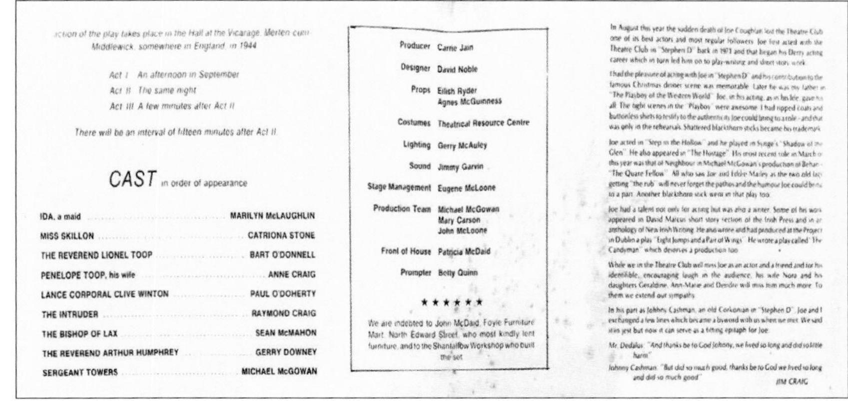

...ction of the play takes place in the Hall at the Vicarage, Merton cum Middlewick, somewhere in England, in 1944

Act I An afternoon in September
Act II The same night
Act III A few minutes after Act II

There will be an interval of fifteen minutes after Act II

CAST in order of appearance

| | |
|---|---|
| IDA, a maid | MARILYN McLAUGHLIN |
| MISS SKILLON | CATRIONA STONE |
| THE REVEREND LIONEL TOOP | BART O'DONNELL |
| PENELOPE TOOP, his wife | ANNE CRAIG |
| LANCE CORPORAL CLIVE WINTON | PAUL O'DOHERTY |
| THE INTRUDER | RAYMOND CRAIG |
| THE BISHOP OF LAX | SEAN McMAHON |
| THE REVEREND ARTHUR HUMPHREY | GERRY DOWNEY |
| SERGEANT TOWERS | MICHAEL McGOWAN |

| | |
|---|---|
| Producer | Carrie Jain |
| Designer | David Noble |
| Props | Eilish Ryder<br>Agnes McGuinness |
| Costumes | Theatrical Resource Centre |
| Lighting | Gerry McAuley |
| Sound | Jimmy Garvin |
| Stage Management | Eugene McLoone |
| Production Team | Michael McGowan<br>Mary Carson<br>John McLoone |
| Front of House | Patricia McDaid |
| Prompter | Betty Quinn |

* * * * * *

We are indebted to John McDaid, Foyle Furniture Mart, North Edward Street, who most kindly lent furniture, and to the Shantallow Workshop who built the set.

In August this year the sudden death of Joe Coughlan lost the Theatre Club one of its best actors and most regular followers. Joe first acted with the Theatre Club in "Stephen D" back in 1971 and that began his Derry acting career which in turn led him on to play-writing and short story work.

I had the pleasure of acting with Joe in "Stephen D" and his contribution to the famous Christmas dinner scene was memorable. Later he was my father in "The Playboy of the Western World". Joe, in his acting, as in his life, gave his all. The fight scenes in the "Playboy" were awesome. I had ripped coats and buttonless shirts to testify to the authenticity Joe could bring to a role - and that was only in the rehearsals. Shattered blackthorn sticks became his trademark.

Joe acted in "Step in the Hollow" and he played in Synge's "Shadow of the Glen". He also appeared in "The Hostage". His most recent role in March of this year was that of Neighbour in Michael McGowan's production of Behan's "The Quare Fellow". All who saw Joe and Eddie Mailey as the two old lags getting "the rub" will never forget the pathos and the humour Joe could bring to a part. Another blackthorn stick went in that play too.

Joe had a talent not only for acting but was also a writer. Some of his work appeared in David Marcus short story section of the Irish Press and in an anthology of New Irish Writing. He also wrote and had produced at the Project in Dublin a play "Eight Jumps and a Pair of Wings". He wrote a play called "The Candyman" which deserves a production too.

While we in the Theatre Club will miss Joe as an actor and a friend and for his identifiable, encouraging laugh in the audience, his wife Nora and his daughters Geraldine, Ann-Marie and Deirdre will miss him much more. To them we extend our sympathy.

In his part as Johnny Cashman, an old Corkonian in "Stephen D", Joe and I exchanged a few lines which became a byword with us when we met. We said it in jest but now it can serve as a fitting epitaph for Joe.

Mr. Dedalus: "And thanks be to God Johnny, we lived so long and did so little harm"

Johnny Cashman: "But did so much good, thanks be to God we lived so long and did so much good"

JIM CRAIG

In the programme notes for Carrie Jain's production of Philip King's See How They Run, staged at Magee College, Jim Craig pens a tribute to TC producer and actor Joe Coughlan, following his sudden death in 1984.

POPPY JUICE THEATRE

PRESENTS

"TILL DEATH DO US PART"

BY

PAMELA BROWN

&

EVA BIRTHISTLE

AT

THE PLAYHOUSE THEATRE

An early stage role at the Playhouse for Performing Arts Academy student Eva Birthistle, who will later go on to work with Ken Loach and win a London Critics Circle award.

Eddie Mailey and his son Stephen study the script.

# Acting pair keep 'All My Sons' in the family

FATHER and son, Eddie and Stephen Mailey, of Londonderry, have plenty in common to talk about these days.

For both are appearing in the Theatre Club's production of Arthur Miller's classic "All My Sons" at Magee College next week.

Eddie, a seasoned local actor, had no difficulty in convincing his ten-year-old son to make his debut in the play which is produced by Gerry McLaughlin.

"He's always been interested in acting and has been helping out backstage on many previous productions," says Mr. Mailey, a teacher at St. Columb's College. "He has appeared in a couple of school productions but is very exited about going on stage with the Theatre Club."

Also appearing in the play will be Jean Feaherty, Maureen Gallagher and Peter Quinn along with newcomers, Jennifer Beattie and Marie O'Keeney.

The show opens at Magee at 8 p.m. on Tuesday, November 27, and runs until next Saturday.

THEATRE CLUB

PRESENT

THE QUEEN AND THE REBELS

BY

UGO BETTI

TRANSLATED BY HENRY REED

LITTLE THEATRE

19th, 20th, 21st, 22nd MAY, 1971

The former Derry City and Northern Ireland footballer Roy Seddon plays a soldier in Denzil Stewart's production of The Queen and the Rebels. (Courtesy Gerry McLaughlin)

William Trevor

Scenes from an Album

Playhouse, Artillery St.

7 - 9 May 1992

Theatre Club

Four members of the Craig family, Johnny, Marianne, Jim and Ann are involved in this production of William Trevor's first drama, Scenes from an Album, along with the BBC's Marie-Louise Kerr (Muir).

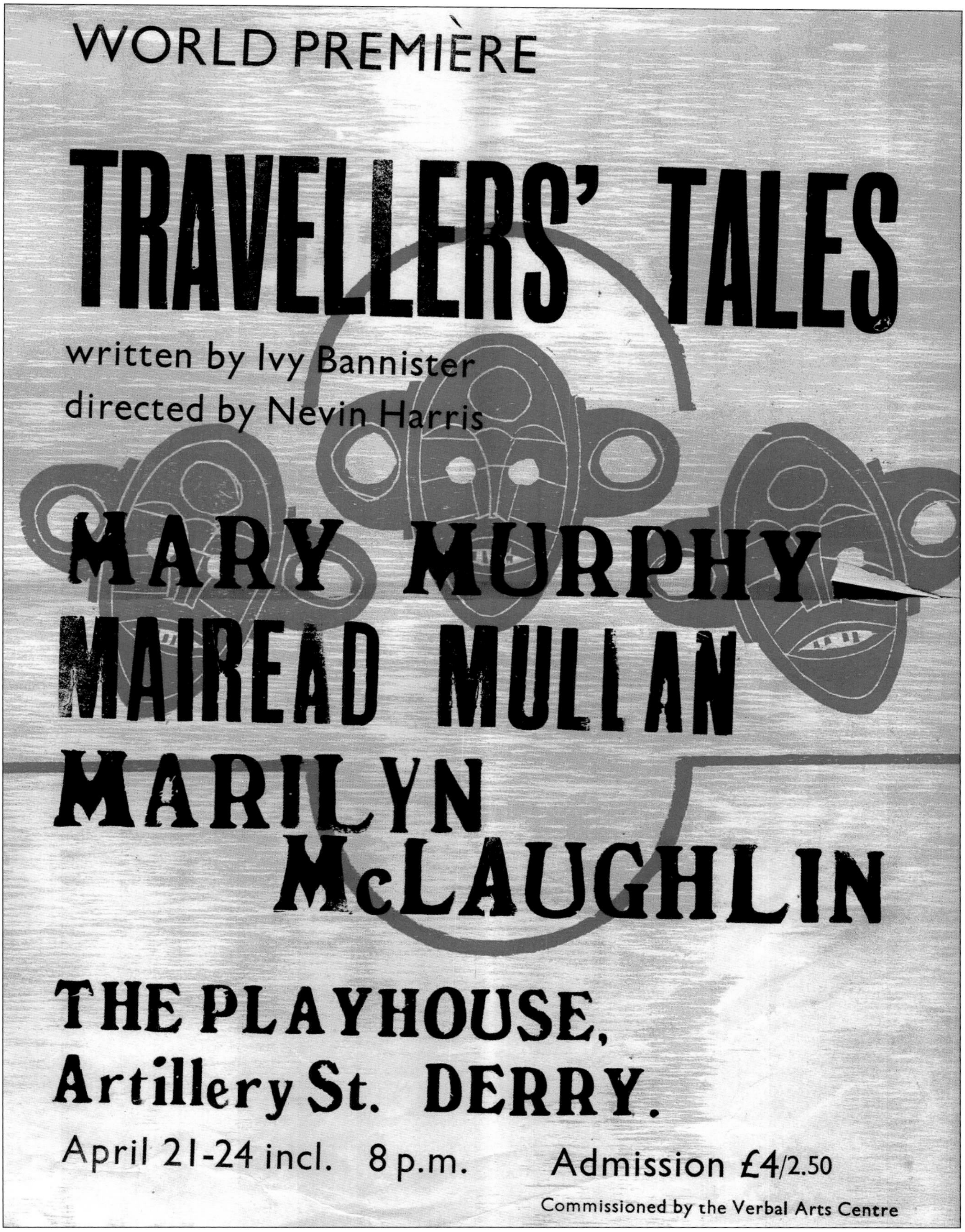

WORLD PREMIÈRE

TRAVELLERS' TALES

written by Ivy Bannister
directed by Nevin Harris

MARY MURPHY
MAIREAD MULLAN
MARILYN McLAUGHLIN

THE PLAYHOUSE,
Artillery St. DERRY.

April 21-24 incl. 8 p.m. Admission £4/2.50

Commissioned by the Verbal Arts Centre

**Dublin poet Ivy Bannister, in residency at the Verbal Arts Centre, is responsible for this three-hander, based on the life of the County Antrim traveller and adventurer Beatrice Grimshaw.**

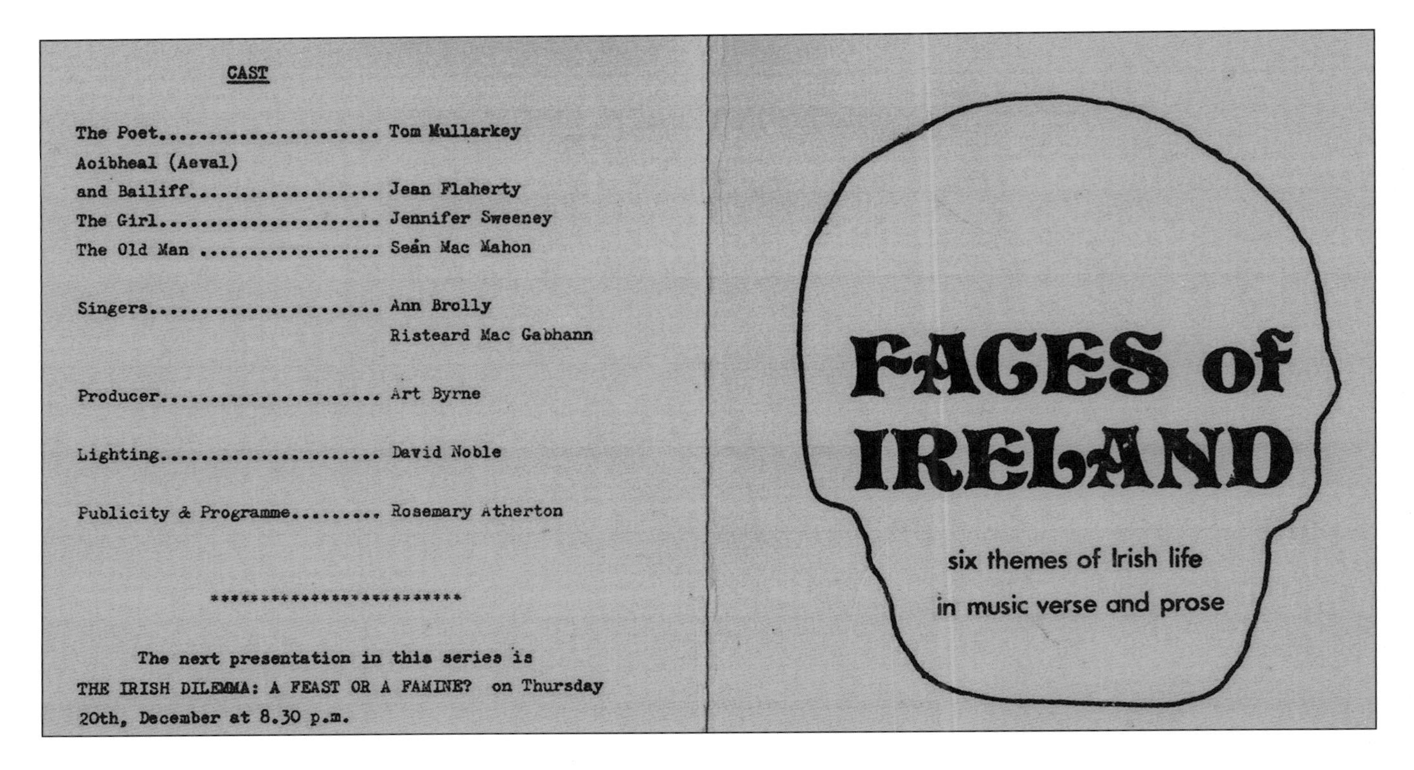

CAST

The Poet.................... Tom Mullarkey
Aoibheal (Aeval)
and Bailiff.................... Jean Flaherty
The Girl.................... Jennifer Sweeney
The Old Man .................... Seán Mac Mahon

Singers.................... Ann Brolly
Risteard Mac Gabhann

Producer.................... Art Byrne

Lighting.................... David Noble

Publicity & Programme......... Rosemary Atherton

**************************

The next presentation in this series is
THE IRISH DILEMMA: A FEAST OR A FAMINE? on Thursday
20th, December at 8.30 p.m.

FACES of IRELAND

six themes of Irish life
in music verse and prose

## INTERMISSION II: FACES OF IRELAND

Sometime in the late 1970s or early 1980s (Derry theatre programmes are notoriously undated), Gerry and several Theatre Club stalwarts teamed up with other dramatists, singers and musicians to produce a series called Faces of Ireland. The troupe would perform an evening of music and readings from Irish writers, themed around a single concept - e.g. The Irish in Love or The Irish at War.

Initially, it was planned to produce six 'Faces', but the evenings proved to be very successful, regularly packing out the Great Hall at Magee. Tours followed, which included performances at the Guildhall and the Riverside Theatre in Coleraine. And as best can be determined, at least nine themed productions were developed.

The players loved doing them as they were guaranteed big houses and didn't have to learn lines. Though a lot of the success was down to producer selection and sharp continuity scripts.

Costumes were also relatively easy to manage, but nothing is entirely foolproof. Jim Craig recalls taking his place with the rest of the cast at the start of a performance, all decked out in a black black uniform. The room went silent in anticipation but, as the lights went up, his mother Maisie announced loudly from the front row: "Oh God, our Jim has odd socks on him!" Craig spent the entire evening with his feet tucked behind the chair.

The Faces team, including Gerry and Seán McMahon, re-assembled for a one-off performance at Derry's Tower Museum in 2007, to mark the 400th anniversary of the Flight of the Earls, during which they read sections from Brian Friel's play, Making History.

PARTICIPANTS

Fear an Tí.................... Bernard Toal

Readers.................... Máiréad Mullen
Mary Murphy
Gordon Fulton

Singers.................... Úna Ó Somacháin
Bernard Heaney
Risteard Mac Gabhann

Musicians.................... Jim Canning
Pádraig Ó Mianáin
Breandán Ó Sandair

Posters and Programme.......... Rosemary Atherton

Lighting.................... Eric Peak

Producer.................... Gerry Downey

PARTICIPANTS

Readers.................... Máiréad Mullen
Mary Murphy
Gordon Fulton
Conner Porter

Singers.................... Úna Ó Somacháin
Dónall Henderson
Risteard Mac Gabhann

Musicians.................... Séamas Ó Canáin
Pádraig Ó Mianáin
Breandán Ó Sandair

Posters and Programme.......... Rosemary Atherton

Lighting.................... Eric Peak

Production and Script.......... Gerry Downey

**************************

The next presentation in this series is:
THE IRISH AND THEIR CREATOR
on Thurs. and Frid. 5-6th. December at 8.00 p.m.

THE IRISH AT WORK AND AT PLAY

Including extracts from the following books and writers:

Kings, Lords and Commons - Frank O'Connor
At Swim-Two-Birds - Flann O'Brien
Gods and Fighting Men - Lady Gregory
Irish Cavalcade - M.J. McManus
Jonathan Swift
Raifteirí
William Carelton
Irish Folk Drama - Alan Gailey
A Book of Ireland - Frank O'Connor
Patrick Gallagher (Paddy the Cope)
Irish Folk Ways - Estyn Evans
Old Irish Street Ballads - James Healy
Cabinet of Irish Literature - Charles Gibbon
Brian Friel
Patrick Kavanagh
Louis McNeice
Seamus Heaney
Seamus Deane
Donagh McDonagh
The Book of Irish Courtesy
Brendan Behan
William Butler Yeats
Oliver St.J. Gogerty
"Derry on the Foyle"
The Tailor and the Ansty - Eric Cross

and the following songs:

The Limerick Rake
An Bacach Buí
The Fair Maid of Comber
An Spailpín Fánach
Casadh an tSúgáin
Fear an Bháta
Galway Races
Rocks of Bawn
McAlpine's Fusiliers
Inis Dhún Rámha
The oul' Trady Quill
One Day for Recreation
The Hot Ashphalt
A Mhuire is a Rí

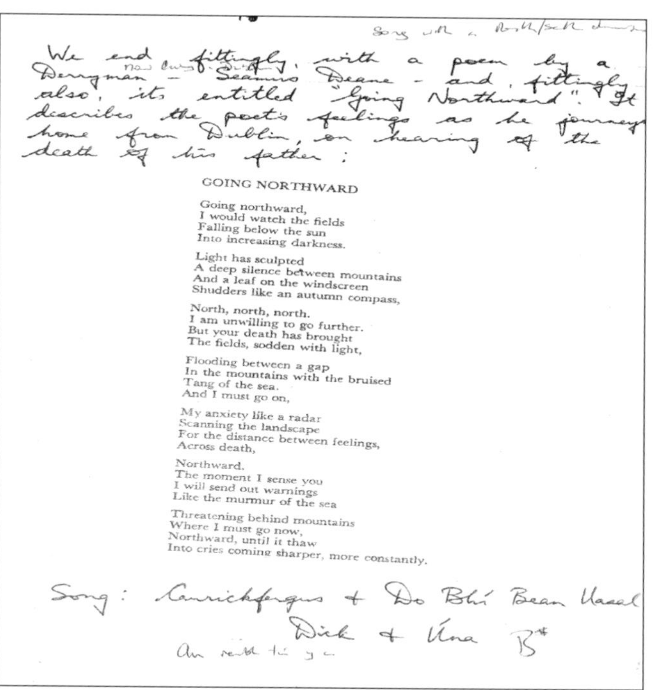

We end fittingly, with a poem by a Derryman – Seamus Deane – and, fittingly also, it's entitled "Going Northward". It describes the poet's feelings as he journeys home from Dublin, on hearing of the death of his father:

GOING NORTHWARD

Going northward,
I would watch the fields
Falling below the sun
Into increasing darkness.

Light has sculpted
A deep silence between mountains
And a leaf on the windscreen
Shudders like an autumn compass.

North, north, north.
I am unwilling to go further.
But your death has brought
The fields, sodden with light,

Flooding between a gap
In the mountains with the bruised
Tang of the sea.
And I must go on,

My anxiety like a radar
Scanning the landscape
For the distance between feelings,
Across death,

Northward.
The moment I sense you
I will send out warnings
Like the murmur of the sea

Threatening behind mountains
Where I must go now,
Northward, until it thaw
Into cries coming sharper, more constantly.

Song: Carrickfergus + Do Bhí Bean Uasal

Gerry was a great admirer of his old school friend Seamus Deane and regularly included his poetry in the Faces of Ireland series - as evidenced here by Gerry's handwritten script (Going Northward is reproduced with the permission of the Deane family.)

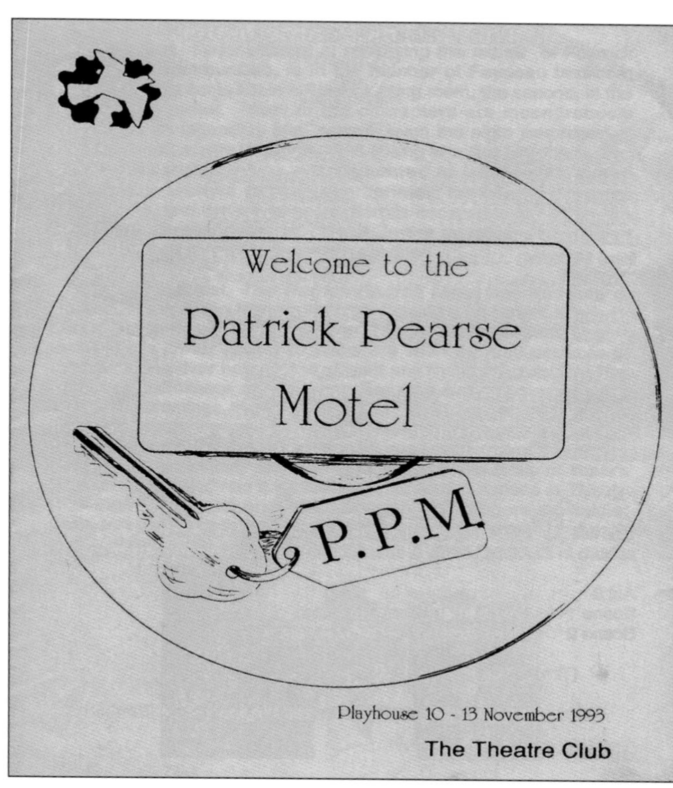



Marie-Louise Kerr (Muir), who will go on to become one of Ireland's top arts broadcasters, makes another TC appearance, this time in the November 1993 reprise of Hugh Leonard's Patrick Pearse Motel.

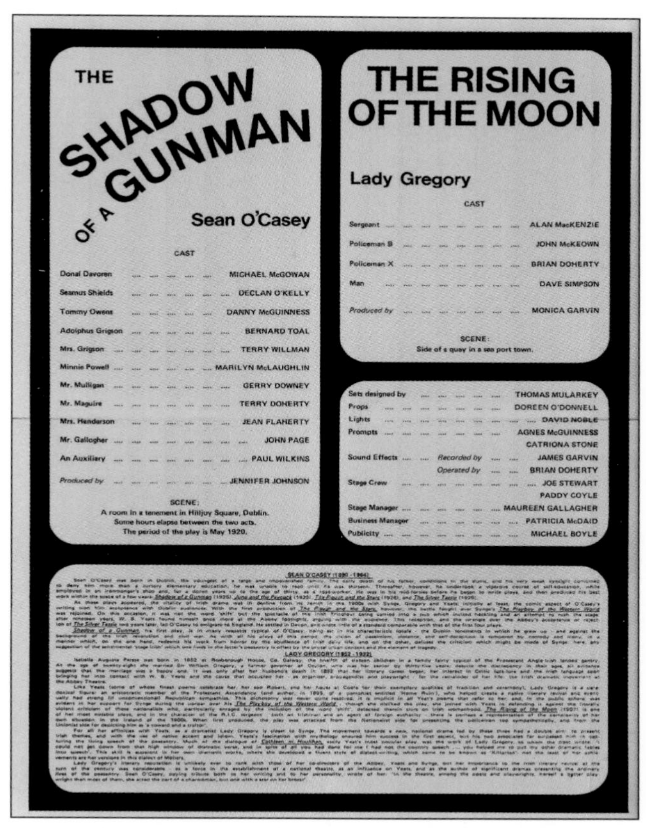

THE SHADOW OF A GUNMAN

Sean O'Casey

CAST

| | |
|---|---|
| Donal Davoren | MICHAEL McGOWAN |
| Seamus Shields | DECLAN O'KELLY |
| Tommy Owens | DANNY McGUINNESS |
| Adolphus Grigson | BERNARD TOAL |
| Mrs. Grigson | TERRY WILLMAN |
| Minnie Powell | MARILYN McLAUGHLIN |
| Mr. Mulligan | GERRY DOWNEY |
| Mr. Maguire | TERRY DOHERTY |
| Mrs. Henderson | JEAN FLAHERTY |
| Mr. Gallogher | JOHN PAGE |
| An Auxiliary | PAUL WILKINS |
| *Produced by* | JENNIFER JOHNSON |

SCENE:
A room in a tenement in Hilljoy Square, Dublin.
Some hours elapse between the two acts.
The period of the play is May 1920.

THE RISING OF THE MOON

Lady Gregory

CAST

| | |
|---|---|
| Sergeant | ALAN MacKENZIE |
| Policeman B | JOHN McKEOWN |
| Policeman X | BRIAN DOHERTY |
| Man | DAVE SIMPSON |
| *Produced by* | MONICA GARVIN |

SCENE:
Side of a quay in a sea port town.

| | |
|---|---|
| Sets designed by | THOMAS MULARKEY |
| Props | DOREEN O'DONNELL |
| Lights | DAVID NOBLE |
| Prompts | AGNES McGUINNESS<br>CATRIONA STONE |
| Sound Effects — *Recorded by* | JAMES GARVIN |
| *Operated by* | BRIAN DOHERTY |
| Stage Crew | JOE STEWART<br>PADDY COYLE |
| Stage Manager | MAUREEN GALLAGHER |
| Business Manager | PATRICIA McDAID |
| Publicity | MICHAEL BOYLE |

SEAN O'CASEY (1880 - 1964)

LADY GREGORY (1852 - 1932)

The Dublin-born novelist Jennifer Johnston, whose mother was a professional director and father was an actor, produced at least three plays for the Theatre Club during the 1970s, (Shadow of a Gunman, The Hostage and one of her own), and was also an advisor to the Theatre Action Group.

THE VISIT

BY

FRIEDRICH DÜRRENMATT

LITTLE THEATRE
10th-14th
April, 1973

Produced by DENZIL STEWART

First published in 1956, this play is generally regarded as Dürrenmatt's masterpiece, though some might argue for The Physicists. Along with Frisch, another Swiss, Durrenmatt is probably the most important dramatist writing in German.

He is inclined to discount the significance of the events of his life - he has said, "I have no biography" - but he has thought it worth including an unmistakable description of himself as a young man, and an indication of his awareness of the nightmare quality of much modern life, in one of his short stories - The Tunnel. He was born in 1921 in Konolfingen, near Berne, the son of a Protestant pastor and this background has been significant in his development. He attended lectures, intermittently, at university, but never graduated. Much of his time was spent in painting and sketching and this training enhanced his descriptive powers. Few dramatists have given more exhaustive indications of scene requirements.

His early plays were expressionist in style, but there was an evolution towards what was to become his particular medium - satirical comedy. With increasing maturity a deepening can be detected in his satire. In the earlier works it had been more general and playful in castigating the petit bourgeois aspects of society. Later it became more profound, more pungent, in beginning to turn its attention to the real ills of the world, such as the chase after prosperity to the exclusion of all else.

The principal theme of his work is the problem of justice and guilt, the mode of expression most natural to him is satire and the means he employs is the grotesque. He probes into the relativity of all justice and guilt. He continually stresses the point that individual guilt no longer applies to our time, which only experiences collective guilt. In his theoretical treatise - Theaterprobleme - he gives this as his reason for writing comedy rather than tragedy - "Tragedy presupposes individual guilt.......... and responsibility." Who is "guilty" in The Visit? Is it Ill (incidentally an example of what is called a "sprechender Name" - a speaking name - another is Güllen, from Gülle meaning liquid manure)? Is it Claire's former lover, whose perjury has precipitated her into a life of vice, and whose execution she has returned to demand as the price of the injection of capital which will transform her native town from an impoverished ruin into a prosperous place? Or is it the citizens who succumb to subconscious promptings which lead them to stifle their sense of justice and humanity in their greed to share in the boom?

V. BRENNAN.

VISITORS

| | |
|---|---|
| Claire Zachanassian, nee Wascher<br>Multi-millionairess, American Oil | PHILIPPA RUSSELL |
| Her Husbands, VII - IX | Bob McKi[illegible]<br>Colm O Donnell |
| Butler | ~~KEVIN MULLAN~~ |
| Toby ) gum-chewers | PETER MULLAN |
| Roby ) | EDDIE MAILEY |
| Koby ) blind | EAMONN GALLAGHER |
| ~~Loby~~ ) | |

VISITED

| | |
|---|---|
| Ill | GORDON FULTON |
| His Wife | THÉRÈSE MARTIN |
| His Son | MAURICE SIMMS |
| His Daughter | MONICA McLAUGHLIN |
| Mayor | GERRY DOWNEY |
| Priest | TOM HAVERTY |
| Schoolmaster | CONNOR PORTER |
| Doctor | LEO McBRIDE |
| Policeman | GERRY McLAUGHLIN |
| Man One | DENNIS GOLDEN |
| Man Two | FRANK O'KANE |
| Man Three | GERRY McLAUGHLIN |
| Man Four, Painter | ROY SEDDON |
| First Woman | ANNE HARVEY |
| Second Woman | MAUREEN O'KANE |
| Miss Louise | Monica McLaugh[illegible] |

EXTRAS

| | |
|---|---|
| Railway Official | EDDIE MAILEY |
| Bailiff | LEO McBRIDE |

DISTRACTORS

| | |
|---|---|
| First Reporter | MARION BYRNE |
| Radio Commentator | KEVIN THOMPSON |
| Cameraman | FRANK O'KANE |
| ~~Photographer~~ | ~~[illegible] MULLAN~~<br>Peter Mullan |

PLACE: GUELLEN, A SMALL TOWN

TIME: THE PRESENT

THERE WILL BE AN INTERVAL OF 10 MINUTES AFTER ACT TWO

| | |
|---|---|
| Production Assistant | PEGGY BOYLE |
| Stage Manager | JEAN FLAHERTY |
| Assistant Stage Manager | DAVID NOBLE |
| Set and Lighting designed by | DAVID NOBLE |
| Assisted by | PHIL CARLIN |
| Lighting | TED GALLAGHER<br>PAT MACDONAGH |
| Sound | MALCOLM McKAY |
| Wardrobe Mistress | MARY HASSON |
| Publicity | ART BYRNE |
| Business Manager | PATRICIA McDAID |
| Secretary | Miss PEGGY BOYLE, 5 LAWRENCE HILL, Tel. 2053. |

The Theatre Club thanks all their patrons and the Management of the Little Theatre who have helped to make last year such a success. We also thank the many business houses who have aided us financially by advertising in our programmes.

Programme designed by DAVID NOBLE and printed by NU PRINT LTD.

The programme notes for The Visit in April 1973 celebrate the club's tenth production.

## ACT III:
## THE '80s AND '90s

*(Exterior: a cast of thousands, decked out in red and white scarves, pours into a football stadium, where Teenage Kicks is blasting from a tannoy.)*

After a harrowing start to the 1980s, Derry started to grow in confidence, due in no small part to the revival of the town's football club, which had been ignominiously shut down by the Belfast authorities in the early '70s. A strong sense of community accompanied Derry City's rise back through the ranks, and this spirit spilled over into wider society. Things were now possible again...

For the first half of the decade, the Theatre Club was still able to average two or three plays a year. Perhaps as a reaction to the tougher times, the company performed a host of comedies and romances, some of which were drawing big audiences. But the club was facing a wide range of challenges – including from the football, which for a time was the only show in town.

One pressing concern was the steady encroachment of 'curriculum development', meaning that teachers, who made up a hefty portion of the club, had less and less free time for outside activities such as drama. Also, the drive by the city's new BBC stadion, Radio Foyle, to produce in-house soaps and dramas, meant that senior Theatre Club players could find themselves drawn to the brighter lights the pros could offer them.

A more telling blow for the club was the loss of the Little Theatre in 1984 after a dispute with the hall's management. The Orchard Street venue had been the club's home for almost a decade-and-a-half and, while the players would soldier on for another decade, it was never quite the same. Magee and the Foyle Arts Centre, while always accommodating, weren't as accessible; the Union Hall wasn't always available – nor was it entirely suitable, and the stage in the Britannia Hall was far too small. Moreover, the Theatre Club had no tradition of touring or competing in festivals, so its outlets for productions were more and more limited.

Most cultural groups were feeling similarly stymied and, by the end of the '80s, the need for purpose-built venues was a huge issue, with organisations such as the

**Art Byrne plays the lead in this 1971 production of Hugh Leonard's Stephen D.**

**The opening of BBC Radio Foyle in 1979 provides a much-welcomed professional outlet for the city's talented performers and producers, including the likes of Joe Mahon, Mickey McGowan, Anita Robinson, Jim and Ann Craig, Seamus Ball and Gerry.**

Musicians' Collective leading the charge for change, assisted by community development champions such as Paddy 'Bogside' Doherty and Conal McFeely.

The opening of the Playhouse at the old convent school on Artillery Street, championed by the dynamic and supportive Pauline Ross, did herald a Theatre Club revival, as did the recruitment of Nevin Harris, an experienced producer and first-class performer, who had recently won the City of Derry Drama Festival Best Actor award for his performance in Macbeth.

Field Day's arrival also energised the city's amateur players, as they flocked to performances and took turns at serving the professional company as ushers, stagehands and taxi-drivers. It was a new and exciting outlet for the younger generation who were keen to pursue professional careers in theatre or the arts.

Gerry continued to direct and act for the Theatre Club, but he was also becoming a sought-after contributor at Radio Foyle. He performed in and wrote soaps, comedies and plays, and he scripted weekly columns for the station's op-ed programme, Comment and Going. He was quick witted and had the ability to ad lib - leading to him getting presenting roles and, for a while, his own series, Murphy's Law. More and more, he was also called on to feed into Radio Ulster's Irish language output. His handwritten radio scripts, many of which he kept, will make yet another fine book.

One satirical series Gerry worked on with the late Thomas McDermott took a light-hearted look at the local political scene. The show was brought to the attention of Gerry's distant cousin, the MP and MEP John Hume, who rang in a very huffy mood to give out to him. Hume hadn't actually heard the show himself, so Gerry, who was playing a character called 'Ron Plume', advised he should give it a listen, as it was all done in the best possible taste. So in fairness, Hume gave it a chance and loved it, and the next time he met Gerry in Cole's Bar he bought him a pint – an honour indeed.

After the former Radio Foyle manager Joe Mahon launched an independent broadcasting company, he would call on Gerry to act in TV dramas and comedies he was making for RTE and the BBC. Gerry's productions with Mahon include the children's series Muintir na Darach/ Secrets of the Oaks, and lead roles in two of the Seanchaí series: as the eponymous Poteen Maker, doing battle with his Theatre Club colleague Mary Murphy; and as The Undertaker, alongside Jim Patton of the 71 Players. Gerry's lifelong friend Dick Mac Gabhann scripted Seanchaí with Mahon, while Theatre Club regular Billy Gallagher was the sound engineer for the series.

This led on to further parts in Irish language TV productions, including memorable roles in the crematorium-based comedy series C.U. Burn (TG4) and as a traditionalist priest in the summer Gaeltacht series Teenage Cics.

Gerry also partnered with Martin Melarkey, Dave Duggan and the new wave of filmmakers in the Nerve Centre, acting in a number of training films with them, and subsequently supplying Irish language voice overs for several of John McCloskey's animated films, including The King's Wake, Cú Chulainn and An Béal Bocht.

He appeared in a number of films too, including Jimmy McGovern's Sunday (as Dr Swords), and Bogwoman, directed by Tommy Collins He did try the world of TV advertising briefly too but was put off the notion when he turned up for an audition only to meet the magnificent Frank Kelly (aka Father Jack) coming out of the studio. No prizes for guessing who got the part.

Film work while easier for line-learning could bring its own hazards. Gerry's Seanchaí co-actor Peter Mullan, a champion swimmer in real life, was required in one scene to play a drowning victim, but ended up spending so much time in the cold water he developed pleurisy and hypothermia. (Or so he insisted. Less sympathetic sources claim there may have been a bit of hypochondria there too.)

When Gerry's former student flatmate, Peter Gallagher (Big Peadar), was appointed head of the North West Institute of Further and Higher Education, he initiated a major expansion programme which saw the 'Tech' estate grow rapidly and expand its ranges of courses. The two men had long shared a common love of drama – Peter had acted with An Craobh – and so decided to establish the Performing Arts Academy. One early success for the new academy was student Eva Birthistle, who subsequently went on to the Gaiety School of Acting, and has won two Irish Film & Television Awards for Best Actress (so far).

Gerry ran the academy until he retired from lecturing in 1997, at which stage he was asked by the University of Ulster to inspect its trainee drama teachers, a job that he revelled in until the travel became too much. As the years progressed, he slipped slowly into full retirement, his last official gig being a weekly Grumpy Old Men column for the Derry News, where he sparred with Kevin Donohoe from the Colmcille Debating Society.

Up until quite recently, Gerry was still penning his immediately recognisable one-line letters to whichever newspaper had infuriated or excited him. (Gerry was the master of pith and could have made a career on Twitter if he wasn't scared to death of all electronic devices.) Sometimes he signed letters with his own name, other times he would make up a nom-de-plume which everyone would see through anyway – Civis Quercus (A Citizen of the Oak) is one that springs to mind. Or, occasionally, for the hell of it, he would simply sign himself 'G. Downey, Derry' to ensure the entire family got the blame. (After a beautiful, listed Victorian building mysteriously fell down and was rebuilt as a glitzy, multi-deck nightclub complex, Gerry responded in the Derry Journal: 'So what's the problem with The Strand Bar, The Strand Bar, The Strand Bar?')

Gerry still went to plays as often as he could (he was captivated but visibly shaken by Sam Shepherd's brilliantly brutal A Particle of Dread in 2013), and he continued to serve as a frequent consultant for An Nua Theatre Company director Paul Moore.

He was delighted to visit the Seamus Heaney Homeplace Centre in South Derry for one of its opening events, and hear his old flatmate Phil Coulter speak with Fr Liam Donnelly and Ambassador Jim Sharkey about their time at St Columb's with the Nobel laureate. Gerry had known Heaney at St Columb's and Queen's, and in 1960 had helped organise a weeklong Cumann Gaelach trip to Rosguill, which the poet took part in and later wrote about in 'The Gaeltacht'. He remembers giving Seamus Heaney and their mutual friend Seamus Deane a lift to Queen's to collect their exam results in the early 1960s – both poets got firsts – and they were all feted with tea and sandwiches at the Heaney family home in Bellaghy on their return.

**Novello-winning John 'Johnny' McDaid, pictured here with song-writing partner Ed Sheeran, has graced stages all around the world with Snow Patrol. He will always be remembered in Derry, however, as a Theatre Club prodigy, who starred in The Tempest at the Britannia Hall in 1992.**

Like the rest of us, the Theatre Club was slowing up but unlike before it had no home base to anchor it. The way in which drama productions (and companies) were financed was increasingly changing, and the club had no access to grants and had no experience in hunting them down.

The late Nevin Harris was the company's final chair and, as his health worsened, the Theatre Club ground to a halt, superseded by a growing band of keen young amateur and semi-professional troupes, many of whom continue to this day.

It was a quiet demise for what had been one of the city's most enduring arts groups. But in many ways it fitted perfectly with Gerry's own gentle and unfussy philosophy of life and theatre, as borrowed from the Bard: "We are such stuff / As dreams are made on, and our little life / Is rounded with a sleep."

It is quite right that the Theatre Club shouldn't be mourned – we should be happy that it lived. But, as Gerry said at the outset, it must certainly be remembered.

**Gerry plays the lead in two episodes of Joe Mahon's darkly comic, bilingual RTE/BBC series, Seanchaí, starring as a money-hungry undertaker in one and a crafty poteen-maker in another.**

**Former Derry drama student Eva Birthistle, who will later work with Ken Loach and win a London Critics Circle award.**

**The Theatre Club continues to struggle to find a new home in the 1990s and attempts a production of The Tempest at the Britannia Hall. The stage, which is about half the size of a dining room table, strains to hold 15 players in the final scenes, and the changing facilities are less spacious again. On the plus side, this February 1992 production features new blood in soon-to-be renowned musicians John McDaid and Paul McLoone (pictured), and pulls full houses. Gerry is cast as Stefano, 'a drunken butler', and wonders if his director, Seán McMahon, might be having a little joke at his expense.**

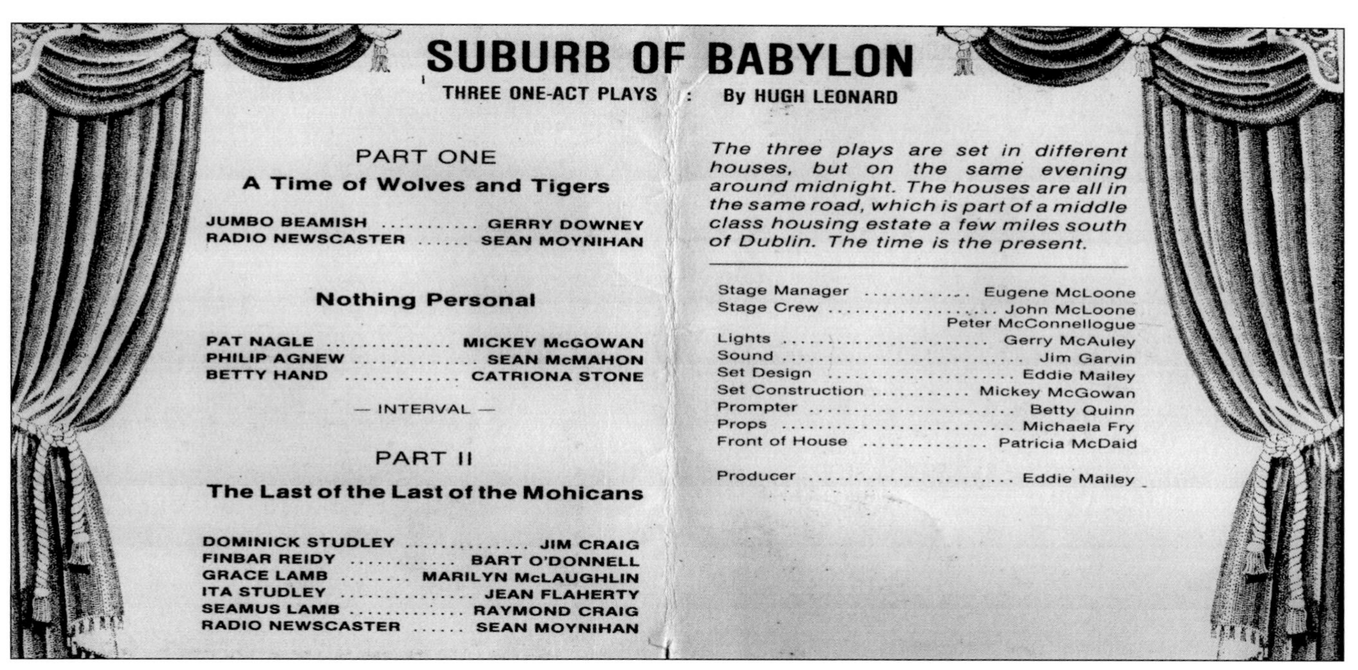

SUBURB OF BABYLON

THREE ONE-ACT PLAYS : By HUGH LEONARD

PART ONE

A Time of Wolves and Tigers

JUMBO BEAMISH ........... GERRY DOWNEY
RADIO NEWSCASTER ...... SEAN MOYNIHAN

Nothing Personal

PAT NAGLE .............. MICKEY McGOWAN
PHILIP AGNEW .............. SEAN McMAHON
BETTY HAND ............. CATRIONA STONE

— INTERVAL —

PART II

The Last of the Last of the Mohicans

DOMINICK STUDLEY .............. JIM CRAIG
FINBAR REIDY ............ BART O'DONNELL
GRACE LAMB ........ MARILYN McLAUGHLIN
ITA STUDLEY ............... JEAN FLAHERTY
SEAMUS LAMB ............ RAYMOND CRAIG
RADIO NEWSCASTER ...... SEAN MOYNIHAN

*The three plays are set in different houses, but on the same evening around midnight. The houses are all in the same road, which is part of a middle class housing estate a few miles south of Dublin. The time is the present.*

Stage Manager ............ Eugene McLoone
Stage Crew ................. John McLoone
Peter McConnellogue
Lights ..................... Gerry McAuley
Sound ........................ Jim Garvin
Set Design .................. Eddie Mailey
Set Construction ........... Mickey McGowan
Prompter ...................... Betty Quinn
Props ........................ Michaela Fry
Front of House .............. Patricia McDaid

Producer ...................... Eddie Mailey

A photograph by Hugh Gallagher of Eamon Friel's Port Pageant, saluting Derry's long history as an emigration port, and starring Jim Craig and Seamus Ball. Other actors in the massive cast include Marie-Louise Kerr, in a singing role, Mickey McGuinness and Gerry (courtesy Hugh Gallagher).

Players in this December 1974 Theatre Club production of Twelfth Night include Mary Murphy, Mairead Mullan, Peter Mullan, Barney Toal and Gordon Fulton (who also directed).

The 1965 Cumann Drámaíochta Chraobh Sheáin Uí Dhubhláin production of An Strainséir Dubh, directed by Fr F. O'Flaherty. Peter Mullan and Therese Martin would both go on to perform with the Theatre Club. Risteard Mac Gabhann (front left) would become an active member of the Theatre Action Group and a director of the Millennium Forum, while Peter Gallagher would become CEO of the North West Regional College and establish the Performing Arts Academy with Gerry (pictured here, centre, in his now customary hat).

Recent arrival from Dublin to Derry, Frank D'Arcy, Magee lecturer and the Irish Independent's literary editor by day, makes an appearance as a priest in this 1974 production of Twelfth Night.

An early role for Mairead Mullan, alongside Mary Murphy, in this 1974 production of Twelfth Night.

Michael Boyle, Mairead Mullan, Connor Porter and Mickey McGowan as the Loman family in this 1976 production of Death of a Salesman.

This photograph of the Freelance Theatre Company meeting Derry mayor Annie Courtney in the early 1990s includes many familiar Theatre Club faces. From left: Nuala Magee (Council Festivals Officer), Jim Patton, Mairead Mullan, Gary McKeone, Niall Coyle, Nevin Harris, and Catríona O'Donnell.

Gerry ponders (unsuccessfully) how to stop Declan O'Kelly wiping his eye in The Promise (1972).

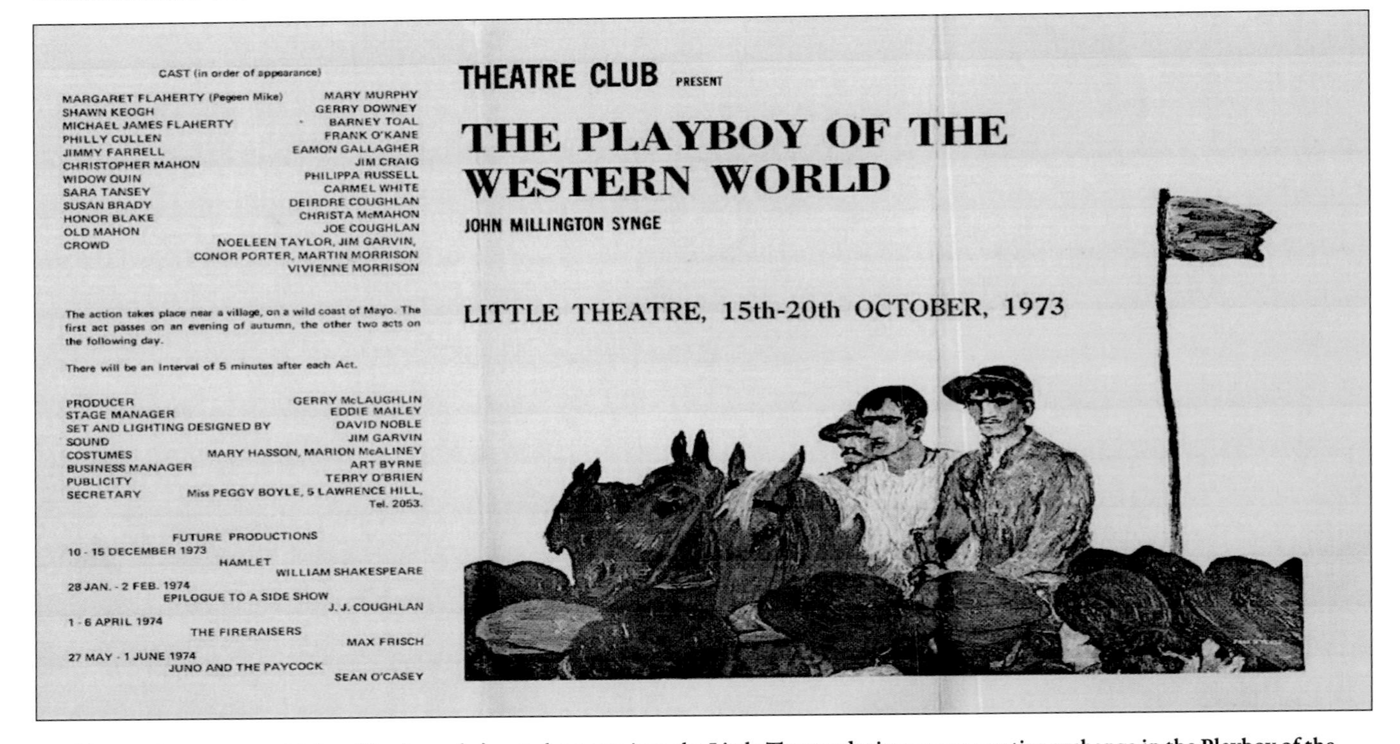

CAST (in order of appearance)

| | |
|---|---|
| MARGARET FLAHERTY (Pegeen Mike) | MARY MURPHY |
| SHAWN KEOGH | GERRY DOWNEY |
| MICHAEL JAMES FLAHERTY | BARNEY TOAL |
| PHILLY CULLEN | FRANK O'KANE |
| JIMMY FARRELL | EAMON GALLAGHER |
| CHRISTOPHER MAHON | JIM CRAIG |
| WIDOW QUIN | PHILIPPA RUSSELL |
| SARA TANSEY | CARMEL WHITE |
| SUSAN BRADY | DEIRDRE COUGHLAN |
| HONOR BLAKE | CHRISTA McMAHON |
| OLD MAHON | JOE COUGHLAN |
| CROWD | NOELEEN TAYLOR, JIM GARVIN, CONOR PORTER, MARTIN MORRISON VIVIENNE MORRISON |

The action takes place near a village, on a wild coast of Mayo. The first act passes on an evening of autumn, the other two acts on the following day.

There will be an Interval of 5 minutes after each Act.

| | |
|---|---|
| PRODUCER | GERRY McLAUGHLIN |
| STAGE MANAGER | EDDIE MAILEY |
| SET AND LIGHTING DESIGNED BY | DAVID NOBLE |
| SOUND | JIM GARVIN |
| COSTUMES | MARY HASSON, MARION McALINEY |
| BUSINESS MANAGER | ART BYRNE |
| PUBLICITY | TERRY O'BRIEN |
| SECRETARY | Miss PEGGY BOYLE, 5 LAWRENCE HILL, Tel. 2053. |

FUTURE PRODUCTIONS

10 - 15 DECEMBER 1973
HAMLET
WILLIAM SHAKESPEARE

28 JAN. - 2 FEB. 1974
EPILOGUE TO A SIDE SHOW
J. J. COUGHLAN

1 - 6 APRIL 1974
THE FIRERAISERS
MAX FRISCH

27 MAY - 1 JUNE 1974
JUNO AND THE PAYCOCK
SEAN O'CASEY

THEATRE CLUB PRESENT

THE PLAYBOY OF THE WESTERN WORLD

JOHN MILLINGTON SYNGE

LITTLE THEATRE, 15th-20th OCTOBER, 1973

The gentleman street drinker, 'Gackawacka', somehow gets into the Little Theatre during a very emotive exchange in the Playboy of the Western World. He begins ad-libbing with the cast, throwing the players into considerable confusion and the audience into hysterics.

Cass Maguire marks the first appearance of David Noble's signature A3 folded card programme.

Jennifer Johnston directs this 1976 production of The Hostage.

# EPILOGUE:
# ENCORE AND GOODBYE

*(A group of older players gather around a large dining table for a reunion dinner. There are lots of stories. Some familiar faces are missing, but they are remembered with great fondness. And there is laughter. Lots of long, happy laughter.)*

There had been no plans for this booklet to have an epilogue, but the wonderful Jean Flaherty's 90th birthday celebrations put paid to that. The day after the party, which was naturally attended by many of her Theatre Club friends, eminent producer Gerry McLaughlin arrived at the Colmcille Press office, armed with a wealth of new memories and invaluable old material.

McLaughlin, it emerged, was the club's secret archivist, without whom we might have no complete list of plays - or any real records at all - just a random bunch of programmes and clippings, all with the dates missing. Within the space of two hours, he was able to improve (and correct) so much of the original manuscript, revise captions and leave the (already-set) Dramatis Personae, presently at 250-plus names, looking desperately incomplete.

He was able to provide proof positive – if such were needed – that one of Derry's greatest living actresses, Brónagh Gallagher, began her career as a Theatre Club ingénue. The St Mary's College teen was cast by McLaughlin in the Theatre Club's production of Hugh Leonard's Time Was in 1986 - tap-dancing to the stage from the back of the hall at the end of the show to sing the audience home.

**The much-loved, and highly experienced, Reggie Smith directs the Theatre Club's production of Hamlet, with Gerry as his number two.**

And he also provided us with one of greatest stories ever told about their old contenders in the 71 Players. Apparently, one night after a show in Dungiven the eight-strong Derry troupe went back to a big refectory for the supper they'd been promised. But as they entered they saw tea and sandwiches to all sides of them – everywhere you could look – enough to feed an army. They were baffled. The apologetic catering lady explained: "We were told to expect 71 players..."

McLaughlin kindly agreed to share his own materials by way of an encore here, to allow us to meet our deadlines. But future versions of this book will incorporate it, and his memories, in a much more coherent and complete fashion.

In the course of compiling this book, it became clear there were sad stories too – it wasn't always possible to stop the outside world from encroaching. On at least one occasion, a player was taken out of rehearsals to be told of the (troubles-related) death of a loved one. Two fellow amateur dramatists were killed in the city during the 1970s. Shows and rehearsals were regularly interrupted by bomb alerts, riots and gunfire. But as founder Seán McMahon said, they never once dreamed of folding, it was their duty to continue.

"We took it seriously," says Gerry McLaughlin. 'We were amateurs in the sense that we didn't get paid, but we were never amateurish."

Gerry Downey stayed with the club to the very end, directing a young Marie Louise Kerr in one of its last productions, a reprise of The Patrick Pearse Motel at the Playhouse in 1993. (He had previously proven a star turn in the comic role of the caretaker, Hoolihan, in Eddie Mailey's version in March 1979.)

What you won't get in any book – though the Derry public will remember – is that most of the Theatre Club productions were of a high quality. A very, very high quality. They could have stood toe-to-toe against the professionals in Dublin or Belfast.

The players, likewise, always gave their all. For the twenty-plus years Gerry was with the Theatre Club, he loved every minute. He lived and breathed every single production. As did his friends. And most importantly of all, they never once failed to take to the stage when others did not. Maybe they were the real pros all along.

*(Lights dim while players take one last bow. Exeunt.)*

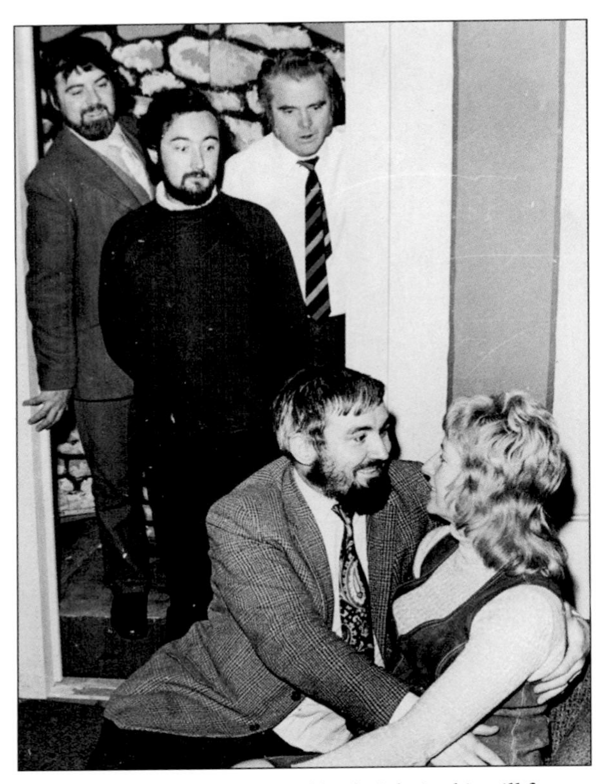

The late Joe Coughlan, pictured back right in this still from Step-in-the-Hollow, is said to have served in the SAS as a young man.

The Foyle Arts Centre on Lawrence Hill is the venue for two plays in Spring year unspecified, (date not recorded either on any of the overall lists, though is post-1988). Brian O'Connor directs Drama at Inish, while Art Byrne is in the chair for Waiting for Godot.

Actor Michael Boyle recalls one night in the early 1970s, while he was on stage pretending to watch a fire, looking out the side window of the theatre where he could see flames ravaging a nearby Foyle Street hotel, which had been targeted in an arson attack.

Mary Murphy and Barney Toal in this still from Lovers (1971)

**Jim Craig impresses the locals with tales of his derring-do in the Playboy of the Western World (1973).**

**A barely-recognisable Gerry McLaughlin looking very dangerous (in beard and shades) alongside Eamon Fitzpatrick, Eddie Mailey, Mickey McGowan and Caitriona Stone in Jennifer Johnston'ss production of The Hostage (1976).**

Four plays in one night in December 1978 - three Pinter shorts and Tom Stoppard's The Real Inspector Hound. Eamon Martin, now Archbishop, provides trombone accompaniment, or as he says himself 'a blast for the cast'.

Director Peter Mullan looks like he is tearing his hair out during this 1976 production of Arthur Miller's Death of a Salesman...

The Theatre Club is a regular supporter of the North West Arts Festival, on this occasion staging The Devil a Saint Would Be at Magee Great Hall, as part of the 1979 programme.

A still from the memorable 1977 Maria Marten: Murder in the Red Barn drama plus Victorian music hall show, produced by Gerry Downey.

**ALL MY SONS** By ARTHUR MILLAR

| | |
|---|---|
| JOE KELLER | EDDIE MAILEY |
| KATE KELLER | JEAN FLAHERTY |
| CHRIS KELLER | PETER QUINN |
| ANN DEEVER | MAUREEN GALLAGHER |
| GEORGE DEEVER | NOEL O'DONNELL |
| DR. JIM BAYLISS | PAUL O'DOHERTY |
| SUE BAYLISS | JENNIFER BEATTIE |
| FRANK LUBEY | JIM CRAIG |
| LYDIA LUBEY | MARIE O'KEENEY |
| BERT | STEPHEN MAILEY |

ACT 1: The back yard of the Keller home in the outskirts of an American town. Early Sunday morning, shortly after the Second World War.

ACT 2: Evening of the same day.

ACT 3: Two o'clock the following morning.

THERE WILL BE AN INTERVAL OF TEN MINUTES AFTER THE FIRST ACT

Arthur Miller was born in New York in 1915. His family was of Austrian Jewish origin. The family fortunes failed in 1931 and Miller grew up in poverty. He worked his way through Michigan University and took a degree in economics and history. He also took a course in play-writing and won three major prizes. On graduating in 1938 he earned his living writing radio scripts. His first successful stage play was "All My Sons", which won the New York Critics Circle Award in 1947. "Death of a Salesman" (1949) established him as a major dramatist, and this and "The Crucible" (1953) are now acknowledged classics of the modern theatre.

| | |
|---|---|
| STAGE MANAGER | EUGENE McLOONE |
| SET | DAVID NOBLE, MICKEY McGOWAN, SHANTALLOW WORKSHOP |
| COSTUMES | CLAIRE TOLAND, MARILYN McLAUGHLIN |
| LIGHTING | JOE STEWART |
| PROPS. | AGNES McGUINNESS |
| FRONT OF HOUSE | PATRICIA McDAID |
| PRODUCER | GERRY McLAUGHLIN |

**Eddie Mailey and son Stephen team up onstage for Gerry McLaughlin's1984 production of All My Sons.**

**The cast of this production of I Do Not Like Thee Doctor Fell includes Michael Gillen, Connor Porter, Mairead Mullan and Monica Garvin (not pictured).**

**Eddie Mailey is never better than as Chief Bromden in Gerry McLaughlin's 1983 production of One Flew Over the Cuckoo's Nest.**

**BBC journalist Marie Louise Kerr (standing far left) takes the stage in this Freelance Theatre Company production of Michael Frayn's Noises Off in the early 1990s. Included are Seamus Ball, Tony McKeown, George McIntyre, Catriona O'Donnell, Jean Flaherty, Mairead Mullan and Gary McKeone.**

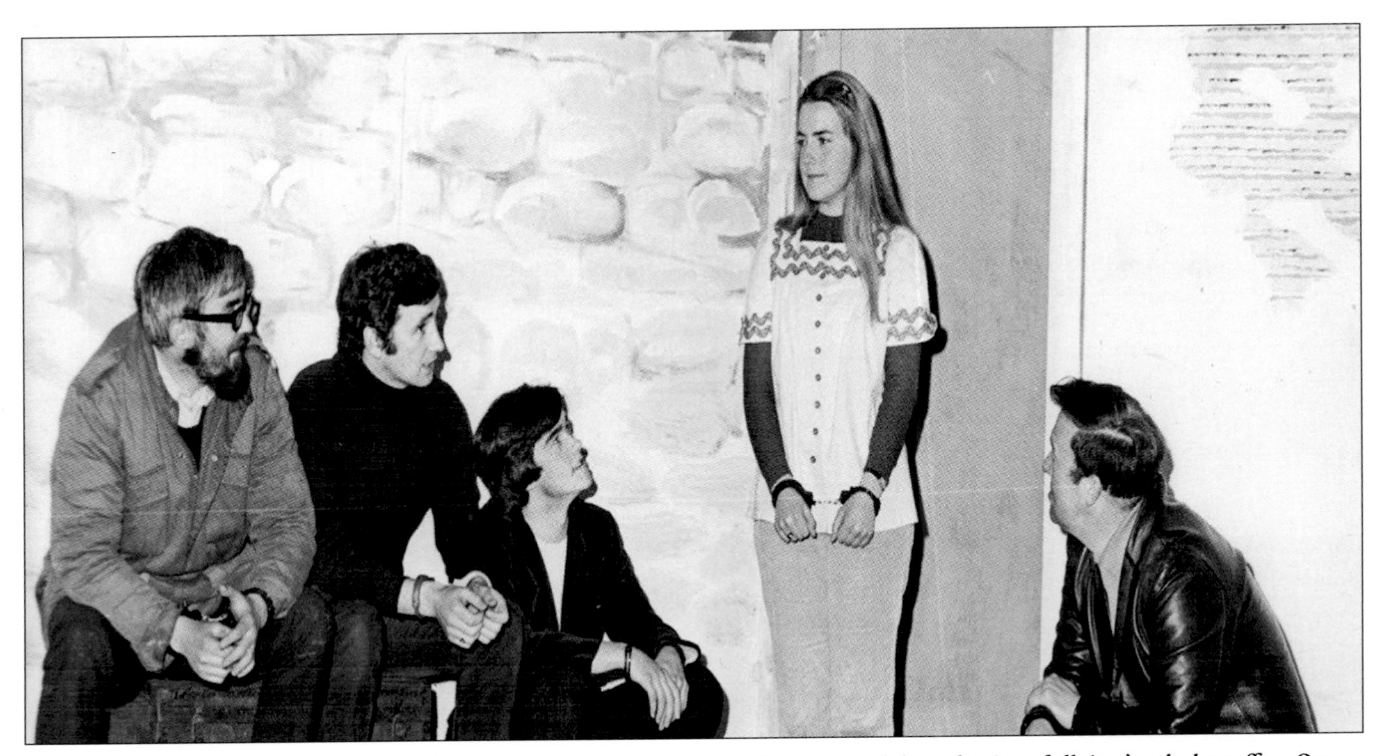

**Sartre's weighty Men Without Shadows is remembered as 'the least successful Theatre Club production of all time' at the box office. One younger player remarks that the club seniors - mostly school teachers - are so busy trying to educate audiences that they end up educating empty seats instead. (He is told to stand in the corner.)**

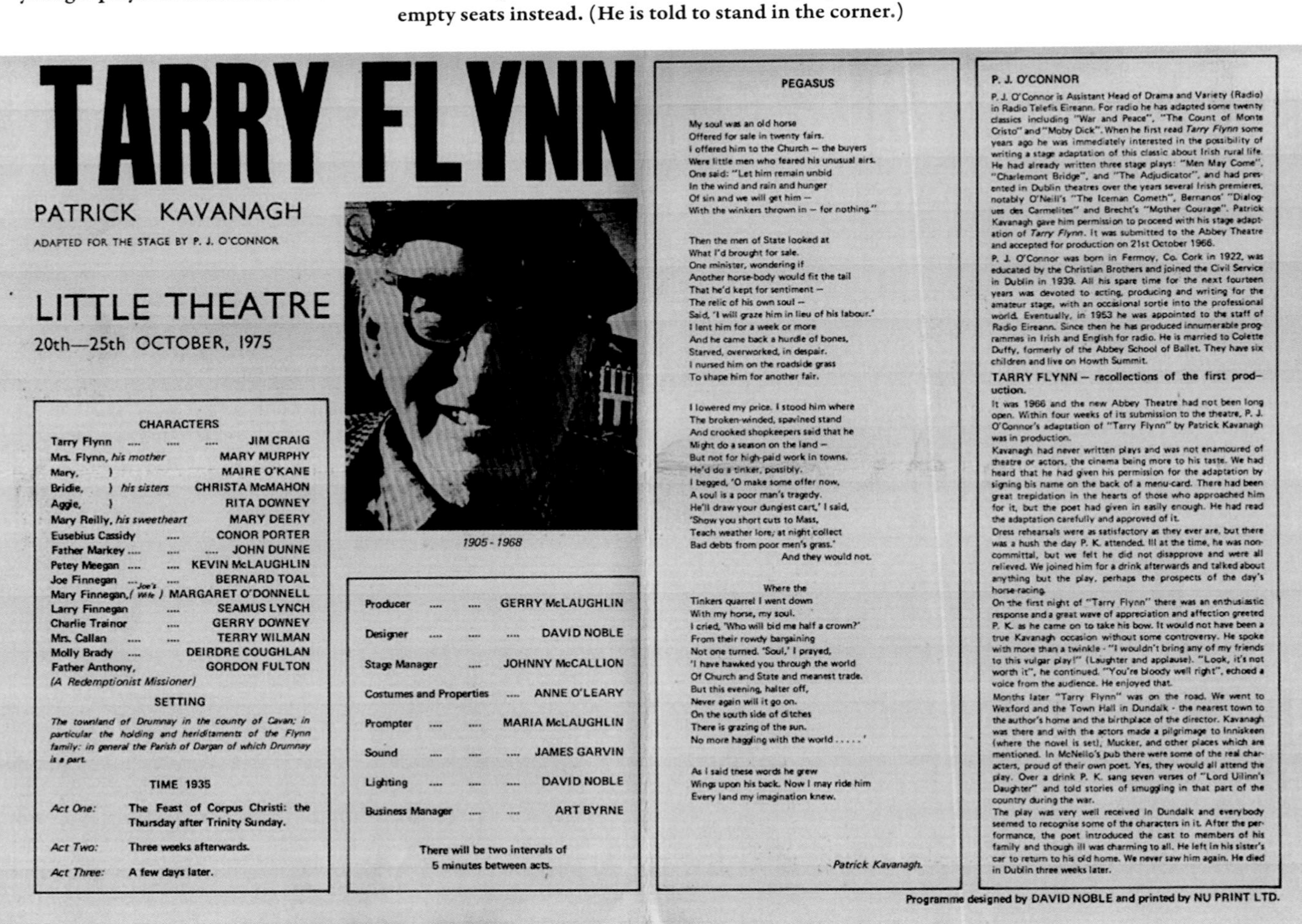

# TARRY FLYNN

PATRICK KAVANAGH

ADAPTED FOR THE STAGE BY P. J. O'CONNOR

LITTLE THEATRE

20th—25th OCTOBER, 1975

1905 - 1968

**CHARACTERS**

|  |  |
|---|---|
| Tarry Flynn .... .... .... | JIM CRAIG |
| Mrs. Flynn, *his mother* | MARY MURPHY |
| Mary, ) | MAIRE O'KANE |
| Bridie, ) *his sisters* | CHRISTA McMAHON |
| Aggie, ) | RITA DOWNEY |
| Mary Reilly, *his sweetheart* | MARY DEERY |
| Eusebius Cassidy .... | CONOR PORTER |
| Father Markey .... .... .... | JOHN DUNNE |
| Petey Meegan .... .... | KEVIN McLAUGHLIN |
| Joe Finnegan .... .... | BERNARD TOAL |
| Mary Finnegan, ( Joe's Wife ) | MARGARET O'DONNELL |
| Larry Finnegan .... | SEAMUS LYNCH |
| Charlie Trainor .... | GERRY DOWNEY |
| Mrs. Callan .... .... | TERRY WILMAN |
| Molly Brady .... | DEIRDRE COUGHLAN |
| Father Anthony, *(A Redemptionist Missioner)* | GORDON FULTON |

**SETTING**

*The townland of Drumnay in the county of Cavan; in particular the holding and heriditaments of the Flynn family; in general the Parish of Dargan of which Drumnay is a part.*

**TIME 1935**

*Act One:* The Feast of Corpus Christi: the Thursday after Trinity Sunday.

*Act Two:* Three weeks afterwards.

*Act Three:* A few days later.

| | |
|---|---|
| Producer .... .... | GERRY McLAUGHLIN |
| Designer .... .... .... | DAVID NOBLE |
| Stage Manager .... | JOHNNY McCALLION |
| Costumes and Properties .... | ANNE O'LEARY |
| Prompter .... .... | MARIA McLAUGHLIN |
| Sound .... .... .... | JAMES GARVIN |
| Lighting .... .... .... | DAVID NOBLE |
| Business Manager .... .... | ART BYRNE |

There will be two intervals of 5 minutes between acts.

**PEGASUS**

My soul was an old horse
Offered for sale in twenty fairs.
I offered him to the Church — the buyers
Were little men who feared his unusual airs.
One said: "Let him remain unbid
In the wind and rain and hunger
Of sin and we will get him —
With the winkers thrown in — for nothing."

Then the men of State looked at
What I'd brought for sale.
One minister, wondering if
Another horse-body would fit the tail
That he'd kept for sentiment —
The relic of his own soul —
Said, 'I will graze him in lieu of his labour.'
I lent him for a week or more
And he came back a hurdle of bones,
Starved, overworked, in despair.
I nursed him on the roadside grass
To shape him for another fair.

I lowered my price. I stood him where
The broken-winded, spavined stand
And crooked shopkeepers said that he
Might do a season on the land —
But not for high-paid work in towns.
He'd do a tinker, possibly.
I begged, 'O make some offer now,
A soul is a poor man's tragedy.
He'll draw your dungiest cart,' I said,
'Show you short cuts to Mass,
Teach weather lore; at night collect
Bad debts from poor men's grass.'
And they would not.

Where the
Tinkers quarrel I went down
With my horse, my soul.
I cried, 'Who will bid me half a crown?'
From their rowdy bargaining
Not one turned. 'Soul,' I prayed,
'I have hawked you through the world
Of Church and State and meanest trade.
But this evening, halter off,
Never again will it go on.
On the south side of ditches
There is grazing of the sun.
No more haggling with the world . . . . .'

As I said these words he grew
Wings upon his back. Now I may ride him
Every land my imagination knew.

-*Patrick Kavanagh.*

**P. J. O'CONNOR**

P. J. O'Connor is Assistant Head of Drama and Variety (Radio) in Radio Telefis Eireann. For radio he has adapted some twenty classics including "War and Peace", "The Count of Monte Cristo" and "Moby Dick". When he first read *Tarry Flynn* some years ago he was immediately interested in the possibility of writing a stage adaptation of this classic about Irish rural life. He had already written three stage plays: "Men May Come", "Charlemont Bridge", and "The Adjudicator", and had presented in Dublin theatres over the years several Irish premieres, notably O'Neill's "The Iceman Cometh", Bernanos' "Dialogues des Carmelites" and Brecht's "Mother Courage". Patrick Kavanagh gave him permission to proceed with his stage adaptation of *Tarry Flynn*. It was submitted to the Abbey Theatre and accepted for production on 21st October 1966.

P. J. O'Connor was born in Fermoy, Co. Cork in 1922, was educated by the Christian Brothers and joined the Civil Service in Dublin in 1939. All his spare time for the next fourteen years was devoted to acting, producing and writing for the amateur stage, with an occasional sortie into the professional world. Eventually, in 1953 he was appointed to the staff of Radio Eireann. Since then he has produced innumerable programmes in Irish and English for radio. He is married to Colette Duffy, formerly of the Abbey School of Ballet. They have six children and live on Howth Summit.

**TARRY FLYNN — recollections of the first production.**

It was 1966 and the new Abbey Theatre had not been long open. Within four weeks of its submission to the theatre, P. J. O'Connor's adaptation of "Tarry Flynn" by Patrick Kavanagh was in production.

Kavanagh had never written plays and was not enamoured of theatre or actors, the cinema being more to his taste. We had heard that he had given his permission for the adaptation by signing bis name on the back of a menu-card. There had been great trepidation in the hearts of those who approached him for it, but the poet had given in easily enough. He had read the adaptation carefully and approved of it.

Dress rehearsals were as satisfactory as they ever are, but there was a hush the day P. K. attended. Ill at the time, he was non-committal, but we felt he did not disapprove and were all relieved. We joined him for a drink afterwards and talked about anything but the play, perhaps the prospects of the day's horse-racing.

On the first night of "Tarry Flynn" there was an enthusiastic response and a great wave of appreciation and affection greeted P. K. as he came on to take his bow. It would not have been a true Kavanagh occasion without some controversy. He spoke with more than a twinkle - "I wouldn't bring any of my friends to this vulgar play!" (Laughter and applause). "Look, it's not worth it", he continued. "You're bloody well right", echoed a voice from the audience. He enjoyed that.

Months later "Tarry Flynn" was on the road. We went to Wexford and the Town Hall in Dundalk - the nearest town to the author's home and the birthplace of the director. Kavanagh was there and with the actors made a pilgrimage to Inniskeen (where the novel is set), Mucker, and other places which are mentioned. In McNello's pub there were some of the real characters, proud of their own poet. Yes, they would all attend the play. Over a drink P. K. sang seven verses of "Lord Uilinn's Daughter" and told stories of smuggling in that part of the country during the war.

The play was very well received in Dundalk and everybody seemed to recognise some of the characters in it. After the performance, the poet introduced the cast to members of his family and though ill was charming to all. He left in his sister's car to return to his old home. We never saw him again. He died in Dublin three weeks later.

Programme designed by DAVID NOBLE and printed by NU PRINT LTD.

**Gerry McLaughlin produces this October 1975 production of Tarry Flynn, with Jim Craig in the lead role.**

# DRAMATIS PERSONAE

*(This is not a complete list, nor by any means a full account of what our players did or went on to do. It is more accurately a list of people that Gerry knew and worked with. Sincere apologies for any omissions; many programmes, cast/crew-lists and memories no longer exist. It is entirely the editor's responsibility for not getting to grips with Gerry's files earlier, as Art Byrne suggested.)*

Aileen Allen: actor in Stephen D with the Theatre Club.
Anita Armstrong (later billed as Anita Robinson): TC wardrobe mistress, prompter, and reviewer. Acclaimed columnist with Irish News and Derry News. Memoirist, public speaker, debating coach and BBC broadcaster.
Thelma Arthur: appeared in a number of TC plays including The Poker Session. Also a member of the City of Derry Drama Club.
Shaun Austin: photographer, sets and occasional TC player. (Stage credits include Stanley in Death of a Salesman)
Lea Aylett: prompter with TC.
Cora Baker (King): director with TC for The Barber of Seville, 1993.
Noeleen Ball: 71 Players mainstay who also worked with TC as lead actor, producer and wardrobe mistress. Winner of Best Actress award at Ballyshannon Festival, 1978.
Seamus Ball: frequent performer with 71 Players and TC. Actor and set designer. Moved into film with The Best Man (1986), then into radio drama and comedy. Numerous screen credits in both film and TV. Still active.
Ivy Bannister: writer for TC. Her play Travellers was premiered by the company in 1993.
Jennifer Beattie: actor with TC in Arthur Miller's All My Sons, 1984.
Iain Barr: director of the Waterside Theatre, and former student of TC mainstay Gordon Fulton.
Eva Birthistle: studied drama at Derry's Performing Arts Academy in the early 1990s, where she acted, produced and helped establish the student theatre company Poppy Juice. Her early performance in Steel Magnolias at the Great James Street Church is commended by the Derry Journal. Today, an award-winning TV and film actor whose credits include Ken Loach's Ae Fond Kiss (for which Birthistle won the London Critics Circle Actress of the Year award), Brooklyn, Ashes to Ashes, and the Last Kingdom.
Sally Bonner: prompter with TC.
Michael Boyle: owner of a well-known city hair salon, he served as lead actor, producer, PRO and programme sponsor with TC and others. As an actor, 'he hadn't a nerve in his body' - always calm and sure. Stage credits include Willy Loman in Death of a Salesman.
Miss Peggy Boyle: TC Company Secretary, (Tel 2053), and teacher at Steelstown PS.
Bernadette Brady: actor with TC. Performed in The Prime of Miss Jean Brodie, 1983.
Caroline Breslin: actor with TC. Performed in The Prime of Miss Jean Brodie, 1983.
John Broderick: stage management with TC.
Noel Brolly: set design with TC.
Amanda Burton: teen actor with the LHS Drama Society, often loaned out to the all-boys St Columb's DS for musicals. Award-winning TV actor with lead roles in Silent Witness and Waterloo Road.
Denis Bradley: columnist, broadcaster and film producer, whose screenwriting credits include The Best Man and Sunset Heights.
Martin Bradley: respected film critic and publicity with TC.
Martin Bradley: musician and chair of the Millennium Forum, chair of Culture Company, which delivered Derry's City of Culture year in 2013.
Michael Bradley: drama producer with BBC Radio Foyle. Writer, broadcaster, authority on music and lifelong Undertone.
Sidney Buchanan: Londonderry Amateur Operatic Society representative on the Theatre Action Group and editor of the Londonderry Sentinel.
Johnny Burgess: theatre graduate, writer, director and actor with Blue Eagle Productions, Waterside Theatre, Verbal Arts Centre, Echo Echo Dance Co., Sole Purpose, Millennium Forum, Ráth Mór, and many more. Production director of the Walled City Tattoo.
Marty Burke: technical wizard and producer with the Nerve Centre. Tech director for the Bloody Sunday Inquiry.
*Art Byrne: Founder, chair, producer, director, scheduler and lead actor (Stephen D) with the Theatre Club. Preferred directing, modestly claiming: "I was a good speaker, but I couldn't walk and talk at the same time...After Stephen D, it all went downhill!" Bibliophile, raconteur and writer.
Declan Carlin: musical accompanist, genius on piano. Co-editor of the landmark book City of Music: Derry's Music Heritage.
Dermot Carlin: stage design and front of house with TC.
Phil Carlin (later Grant): set design and costume

design.
Tony Carlin: legendary musician and MC, also acted with TC (Merchant of Venice).
Mary Carson: production with TC on See How They Run. Journalist, writer and producer.
Helen Clark: actor with TC in The Tempest, 1992.
*Sean (Barlow) Cassidy: actor/reader with TC before the company began its stage productions.
Tommy Collins: multi-award winning filmmaker, who directed Gerry in Bogwoman (1997).
Maeve Connelly: actor with Gerry and Kevin McCallion in the Derry Halloween Pageant. Drama coach and producer; director of the Thornhill Debating & Public Speaking Society.
Tim Connelly: lead actor with TC, 71 Players and other groups.
Damien Cook: stage management with TC.
Joe Coughlan: actor, director and writer with TC.
Phil Coulter: teen actor and prodigious musical director with St Columb's Dramatic Society. Eurovision-winning and grammy-nominated songwriter. Shared a flat with Austin Currie and Gerry at Queen's.
Sean Courtney: actor, Pinter Trilogy with TC.
Brenda Coyle: actor in the Pinter Trilogy and other plays with TC.
Corinne Coyle: actor with TC. Performed in The Prime of Miss Jean Brodie, 1983.
Louise Coyle: actor in Maria Marten with TC.
Niall Coyle: actor in musicals, in the bilingual TV series Seanchaí, and with the Freelance Theatre Company.
Paddy Coyle: stage management with TC.
Ann Craig (née O'Leary): regular lead with TC, as well as director and stage manager. BBC Irish Language producer and broadcaster. Voice actor. Education Officer with the Millennium Forum, (her voice is still used to remind you to switch off your mobile phone at curtain up). Established the Literary Tour of Derry with her husband Jim.
Jim Craig: Frequent lead actor with TC, the Faces of Ireland troupe and the Banba Theatre Company. Played the lead in the Port Pageant, as St Colmcille opposite Seamus Ball's William of Orange. Active in radio drama, and was a cast member in Radio Foyle's first weekly soap opera, Our Street. Still a seasonal BBC broadcaster.
Johnny Craig: actor with TC in Scenes From an Album, 1992.
Marianne Craig: actor with TC in Scenes From an Album, 1992.
Raymond Craig: actor, performed in several TC productions including The Quare Fella in 1984 and also with Banba Touring Company.
Ann Crilly: founding member of the Foyle Film Festival and the Derry Film and Video Collective. Producer, director and university lecturer.
Gerry Crossan: actor, performed in The Quare Fella with TC in 1984.
Hugo Crumlish jr: actor, performed in The Quare Fella with TC in 1984.
Hugo Crumlish snr: actor, performed in The Quare Fella with TC in 1984.
Tracy Cullen: stage manager with TC.
Vinny Cunningham: film producer whose credits include Teenage Kicks:

**Time Was marks Brónagh Gallagher's Theatre Club debut in 1986, but strangely doesn't earn her a listing in the credits!**

The Undertones, and The Free Derry Story. Film editor and cameraman for the Seanchaí series and numerous other TV dramas and documentaries.
Jim Curran: founder member of the Nerve Centre, Foyle Film Collective and Musicians' Collective. Film maker, musician, DJ, university lecturer and accomplished indoor footballer.
Marie Darcy: actor with TC in The Unvarnished Truth, 1982.
Seamus Deane: award-winning author, poet, critic and Field Day founder. His novel Reading in the Dark (1996) won the Guardian Fiction Prize and the Irish Times International Fiction Prize.
Bernadette Dennis: actor and prompter with TC.
Brian Doherty: actor in Rising of the Moon with TC.
Garvin Doherty: actor in Stephen D.
Ian Doherty: teen lead actor in TC's first stage production, Lovers (Winners). Sponsor and supporter of many North West drama societies.
Mariann Doherty: props with TC.
Patrick Doherty: sound engineer for TC, including The Barber of Seville, 1993
Terry Doherty: actor in Shadow of a Gunman with TC.
Thomas Doherty: producer and actor with the '71 Players. Also performed in and directed musicals.
Roisin Donaghy: actor with TC. Performed in The Prime of Miss Jean Brodie, 1983.
Rory Donaghy: musician and song-writer. Lecturer, producer with the Nerve Centre, and director of Blast Furnace Music Studios at Ráth Mór.
Ursula Donaghy: actor in George with TC.
Brendan Donnelly: actor with TC. Performed in Hugh Leonard's Summer, 1988.
Peter Donnelly: actor in Pinter Trilogy with TC.
Áine Downey: rinceoir, amhránaí agus aisteoir le Compántas Taibhdhearc Bhéal Feirste. Occasional actor and legendary after-party host with TC. Administrator and consultant for Theatre Action Group. Academic and author of the memoir The Mortons Who Spoke Chinese, which would make an excellent radio or TV drama.
Bertie Downey: shoemaker and long-standing purveyor of props and lifts. 'Learned' half the Theatre Club to drive - even taught Anita Armstrong.
Cormac Downey: teen musician with Hillman Imp, cartoonist on two books by Yes Publications. Studied film in Liverpool and once appeared as an extra in C4's Hollyoaks.
Garbhán Downey: missed the acting gene entirely. Served the family as an occasional reviewer and publicist.
*Gerry Downey: actor, producer and founding member of the Theatre Club. Chaired the company and represented it on the Theatre Action Group (as Secretary). Also performed with An Cumann Drámaíochta at Queen's and with An Craobh in Derry. Writer and director of the Faces of Ireland series. Writer and broadcaster with Radio Foyle and Radio Ulster. Numerous radio, film and TV credits in both English and Irish. Voice actor (animation) in An Béal Bocht, Cú Chulainn and the award-winning Kings Wake (Stephen Rea did the English version, Gerry the Irish). Lecturer, drama-teaching inspector, coach, and co-founder of NW Regional College's Performing Arts Academy. Former chair of the North West Arts Association.
Kevin Downey: prompter with TC.
Rita Downey: prompter with TC.
Rónán Downey: multi-award winner in many disciplines at Derry Feis before being recommended by his primary school principal, Mickey Gillen, to the BBC. Starred in the adaptation of Bernad McLaverty's My Dear Palestrina alongside Liam Neeson and Eleanor Bron. Musician, visual artist, writer and beautiful human being.
Pat Duffy: actor, performed in The Quare Fella with TC in 1984.
Dave Duggan: Oscar-nominated writer for his short film Dance Lexie Dance. Founding director, actor and writer with Sole Purpose Productions. Renowned playwright, novelist and commentator in English agus i nGaeilge.
John Dunne: regular player with TC and 71 players. Gerry's cousin. Writer, memoirist and sports broadcaster. Widely remembered as one of the city's most inspiring English teachers.
Maureen Egan: business manager with TC.
Pat Farry: actor with TC. Stage roles include Habeas Corpus.
Eamonn Fitzpatrick: actor with TC.
Jean Flaherty: regular lead actor with TC and the Freelance Theatre Company. Drama coach, festival organiser and judge. One of the originals.
Brian Foster: writer of hit stage plays such as Máire, Woman of Derry, The Butterfly of Killybegs, From the Camp to Creggan and A Miracle in Donegal.
Brian Friel: Tony-winning dramatist who was generous to a fault with TC, allowing the company (via his brother-in-law Seán McMahon) to stage early productions of his newest works. Led campaigns to develop a new theatre and a professional theatre company for the North West (subsequently Field Day).
Eamon Friel, writer of the acclaimed Port Pageant, a musical journey through Derry's emigration history. Musical director on numerous Playhouse productions. Sony-winning broadcaster with BBC Radio Ulster.

Accomplished singer-songwriter and satirist. Much missed.
Michaela Fry: actor and prompter with TC in The Unvarnished Truth, 1982.
Gordon Fulton: huge talent. After many big roles with TC, he forsook a career as an English/Drama teacher at Foyle College to enjoy a professional career acting in TV and film. Dozens of credits including: Taggart, Give My Head Peace, and Game of Thrones.
Brónagh Gallagher: began her distinguished film, TV and singing career at St Mary's Drama Society in Creggan, and with the Oakgrove Drama Group. Numerous screen credits including The Commitments, Pulp Fiction and Sherlock Holmes. Also featured on a postage stamp as part of the Irish Film Centenary series. Remains hugely supportive of the NW arts scene and is Patron of Ráth Mór.
Eamonn Gallagher: lifelong gentleman actor with the '71 Players, Theatre Club and many other Derry troupes, performing in both musicals and dramas. Also appeared in films produced by Terence McDonald and others.
Gavin Gallagher: set design for TC, The Barber of Seville, 1993.
Jack Gallagher: aka Rusty. Chief producer with St Columb's PPU, where he taught, and later with City of Derry Drama Club. 'Knew a lot.' First chair of the Theatre Action Group. He is remembered as a kind and tolerant teacher in an era when some were not.
Maureen Gallagher: actor, stage manager and producer with TC. Festival director, judge and senior BBC producer.
Peter Gallagher (aka Big Peadar): talented player with St Columb's DS and An Craobh, educationalist, FE and RTC college president, and co-founder of the Performing Arts Academy. Flatmate of Gerry's at Queen's.
Margaret Gallagher: co-founder of the Foyle Film Festival, lecturer at Derry's Performing Arts Academy.
Stephen Gallagher: musical director with the Performing Arts Academy.
Ted Gallagher: lighting, photography and occasional small parts with TC.
Jim Garvin: actor and stage manager with TC.
Monica Garvin: actor and producer with TC. Directed The Prime of Miss Jean Brodie in 1983.
Joanna Gavin: front of house with TC.
George Gillen: actor with TC in The Tempest, 1992.
Michael Gillen: lifelong actor and producer with many Derry groups including TC, St Columb's PPU, 71 Players, CDDC. Chair of the Theatre Action Group. Sat on the board of Dublin's Abbey Theatre, and was a regular festival director in Derry and Donegal.
Lucille Gillespie: actor with TC. Performed in The Prime of Miss Jean Brodie, 1983.
Joey Glover: treasurer of the Londonderry Amateur Operatic Society and a member of the CIty of Derry Drama Club. On November 23, 1976 he was shot dead at his Crawford Square office by gunmen said to have been targeting his politician brother. According to Nuala McAllister Hart in her book From Farquhar to Field Day, Glover had been an "accomplished singer, organist, actor and compère of the Guildhall wartime concerts". He had been due to perform in a CDDC production of Antigone, at Magee College on the night of his murder. He was also an avid mountaineer.
Denis Golden: actor in The Visit with TC and The Tempest.
Damian Gorman: author, poet, playwright and screenplay writer, who worked with Gerry on the King's Wake.
Marian Gribbin (later Byrne): actor with the City of Derry Drama Club and TC.
Julius Guzy: actor with the Playhouse Theatre Company. Visual artist.
Margo Harkin: an early member of the Field Day production team. Co-founder of the Derry Film and Video Workshop. Produced Ann Crilly's (banned) film Mother Ireland and the award-winning Hush-a-Bye-Baby (starring Sinead O'Connor). Her film Bloody Sunday: A Derry Diary, charting her personal reflections and experiences, won an IFTA award for best Irish Feature Documentary.
Paul Harrigan: stage management with TC.
Nevin Harris: award-winning actor, director and last chair of TC.
Anne Harvey: actor in The Visit with TC.
Mary Hasson: wardrobe mistress with TC.
Tom Haverty: Galway born actor and set-designer with TC.
Michael Hazelden: actor in Merchant of Venice with TC.
Roseanne Hazelden: actor in Merchant of Venice with TC.
Aidan Heaney: actor with the '71 Players and also the Theatre Club, including Tons of Money, 1981.
Aine Heaney: actor with TC. Performed in The Prime of Miss Jean Brodie, 1983.
Bernard Heaney: singer and musician who performed in the Faces of Ireland series. Toured with the trad folk band Aileach.
Seamus Heaney: teen player with St Columb's Dramatic Society, later remembering his acting contemporaries in the poem The Real Names. Field Day co-founder and playwright. Nobel-winning poet.
Patricia Heaney: singer and performer. Acted with the Playhouse Theatre Company in Maria Marten (Murder in the Red Barn).

Maureen Hegarty (née McGuinness): one of the greatest singers ever from northwest Ireland. Had her own BBC TV series, Sounds Irish, and was a regular on RTE and UTV.
Michael Hegarty: set design with TC.
Patrick Hickey: actor in Stephen D with TC.
Peter Hill: remembered as a talented singer with the Londonderry Amateur Operatic Society. A retired army major from a well-known business family, he was shot dead outside his Limavady Road home in February 1977.
Mary Hinds: player with the '71 Players.
Helen Hutton: actor with TC. Performed in The Prime of Miss Jean Brodie, 1983.
Monique Jacquemot: actor in The Long Christmas Dinner with TC.
Carrie Jain: actor, director and prompter with TC. Stage roles include Habeas Corpus.
Jennifer Johnston: producer of Shadow of a Gunman and The Hostage with TC: 'Held our respect. Knew what she was doing.' Multi-award-winning novelist, shortlisted for the Booker Prize. Her novel Shadows on our Skin was filmed by the BBC in Derry, with Derek Mahon providing the screenplay.
Bridget Keenan: chair and director with TC. Festival director.
Ann Kelly: actor with TC in Death of a Salesman.
Des Kelly: set design with TC.
Allen Kennedy: actor, performed in The Quare Fella with TC in 1984.
Eddie Kerr: playwright, director and teacher. Newspaper columnist, broadcaster and writer/producer of the hugely-popular Derry stage-comedy Packie's Wake.
Carita Kerr: actor with TC in Habeas Corpus. Classically trained singer performing with a wide range of choirs and clubs. Derry Feis winner on many occasions. Chair of the Classical Music Society.
James Kerr: teen actor with St Columb's Drama Society, performing as Bill Sykes in Oliver.
Marie Louise Kerr: actor with TC in Scenes From an Album, 1992, and in The Patrick Pearse Motel, 1993. Arts journalist, TV and radio producer and presenter.
Joe Keys: actor with St Columb's Drama Society, TC and others.
Brian Lacy: Dublin-born academic, archaeologist, and writer. Actor with TC.
Jimmy Larmour: St Columb's Hall caretaker, who lived in an apartment in the building. Responsible, among other things, for lighting the overhead gas heaters in the Little Theatre.

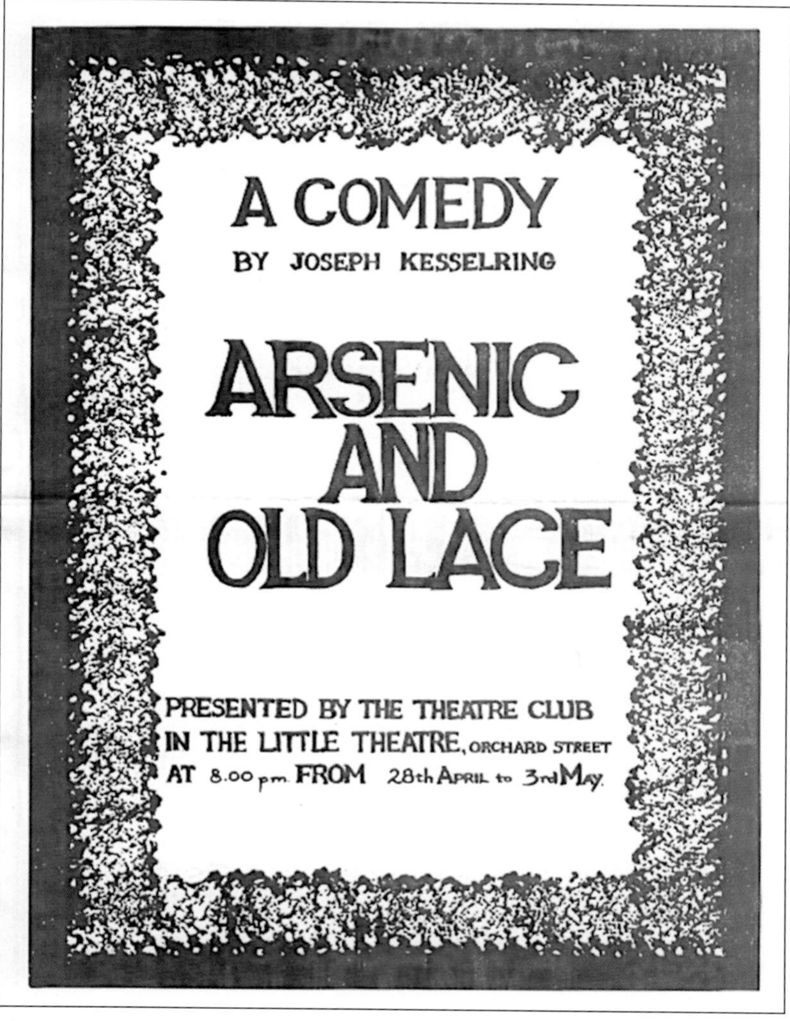


**This 1980 programme advertises the club's annual dinner dance at the Kildrum Country Club - tickets £5.50 from committee members.**

Avril Leach: actor with TC. Performed in The Unvarnished Truth, 1982.
Cathal Logue: Derry Council representative on the Theatre Action Group.
Betty Lynch: prompter with TC.
Pat Lynch: involved in drama at a young age before becoming a stage actor with many Derry theatre companies. Performed in The Quare Fella with TC in 1984. Also a regular screen actor.
Pat MacCafferty: driving force behind Feis Dhoire Cholmcille, the MacCafferty Singers and countless choirs. Acted with the Theatre Club in Stephen D.
Seamus MacCafferty: baritone singer, chorister, and performer. Acted with the Playhouse Theatre Company in Maria Marten.
Joan Mac Gabhann: a wise friend to all and a complete star.
Risteard Mac Gabhann: writer and award-winning musician. Actor and producer with An Craobh, Cumann Cholmcille and the Faces of Ireland troupe

amongst others. Founding member of the Theatre Action Group, later on the board of the Millennium Forum and Cultúrlann Uí Chanáin. Screenwriter for the Seanchaí series.
Alan MacKenzie: actor in TC's Rising of the Moon.
Joe Mahon: inspirational Radio Foyle manager and energetic champion of Derry dramatists, writers and talents. Broadcaster, filmmaker, producer, writer, TV presenter, Bafta-winning director and MC par excellence.
*Eddie Mailey: St Columb's DS and PPU stalwart. Theatre Club founder. Actor, writer, coach, stage manager, raconteur and always-popular producer.
Stephen Mailey: actor with TC in Arthur Miller's All My Sons, 1984. Musician and organist with Trinity College Dublin Chapel Choir.
Una Mailey: poster and programme designer with TC.
Eamon Martin: teen actor with St Columb's DS and trombone-player in the Pinter Trilogy with TC in 1978 inter alia. Primate of All Ireland.
Nóirín Martin: actor and front-of-house with TC.
Sean Martin: actor with TC. Performed in Streetcar Named Desire in 1988.
Thérèse Martin: actor in The Visit with TC.
Leo Marshall: actor with the '71 Players.
Leo McBride: actor in The Visit with TC.
Ciaran McAlister: actor with TC in The Barber of Seville, 1993.
Catherine McCallion: actor with TC. Performed in The Prime of Miss Jean Brodie, 1983.
Carmel McCallion: lead actor, costume designer and stage management with the 71 Players and various other companies. Won widespread acclaim for her performance in Brian Foster's Máire, Woman of Derry. Acted with the Theatre Club in Hugh Leonard's Summer, 1988. Film credits include Bloody Sunday, 2002, in which she played civil rights leader Brigid Bond.
Johnny McCallion: stage manager and company chair with TC.
Kevin McCallion: lead actor with TC, 71 Players. Performed off Broadway in Eddie Kerr's Packie's Wake.
Eamonn McCann: author, broadcaster and teen actor with Gerry at St Columb's DS.
Gerry McCauley: lighting engineer with TC. Founding guitarist with Derry's most notorious punk band, Dick Tracy and The Green Disaster. Still rockin'.
Jack McCauley: actor and stage manager with TC.
Gerry McClelland: lighting engineer with TC.
John McCloskey: artist, book illustrator, musician,

THE
GENTLE ISLAND
by
BRIAN FRIEL

LITTLE THEATRE, Orchard Street
27th January—1st February, 1975

CAST

| | |
|---|---|
| MANUS SWEENEY | EDDIE MAILEY |
| JOE | BOB McKIMM |
| PHILLY | DECLAN KELLY |
| SARAH | DINAH MEIN |
| PETER QUINN | GORDON FULTON |
| SHANE HARRISON | CONOR PORTER |
| BOSCO | EDDIE CAMPBELL |
| TOM | RAYMOND O'DONNELL |
| ANNA | JENNIFER SWEENEY |
| NEIL | JOE O'DONNELL |
| MARY | EDITHA RIDDELL |
| PADDY | REG NORTH |

*There will be an interval of 10 minutes after Act 1.*

| | |
|---|---|
| PRODUCERS | SEAN McMAHON<br>ART BYRNE |
| DESIGNER | DAVID NOBLE |
| LIGHTING | TED GALLAGHER |
| STAGE MANAGER | JOHNNY McCALLION |
| BUSINESS MANAGER | GERRY DOWNEY |

OUR NEXT PRODUCTION 14 – 19 APRIL, 1975.
PURPLE DUST
BY SEAN O'CASEY

Programme designed by DAVID NOBLE and printed by NU PRINT LTD.

**A rare role as Business Manager for Gerry in this production of The Gentle Island.**
**(The company's next billed production, Purple Dust, does not seem to have proceeded.)**

and BAFTA-nominated animator, who cast Gerry in several productions. Celtic Film Festival award-winner. Like Gerry, McCloskey forsook what might have been a lucrative career in professional football for the arts.
Hilary McCloy: production on plays with TC.
Peter McConnellogue: actor, performed in The Quare Fella with TC in 1984.
Paul McCool: actor with TC. Performed in Hugh Leonard's Summer, 1988.
Ken McCormack: writer, historian and playwright. Scripted, produced and acted in dozens of plays for Radio Foyle.
Madeleine McCully: author, creative writing teacher, union representative on the Theatre Action Group.
Charles McDaid: actor, performed in The Quare Fella with TC in 1984.
John McDaid: actor in The Long Christmas Dinner with TC. Regular club sponsor.
John 'Johnny' McDaid: lead roles with St Columb's DS in Guys and Dolls, and Oliver. Teen actor with TC in The Tempest at the Britannia Hall in 1992, before developing his musical genius, joining Snow Patrol and becoming an Ivor Novello-winning songwriter.
Patricia McDaid: business manager and company secretary with TC.
Pauline McDaid: costumes and set designer with 71 Players and others. Artist extraordinary.
Pat MacDonagh: lighting engineer with TC.
Martin McDonald: lighting designer with TC.
Peter McDonald: set designer with TC.
George McDowell: lighting engineer with TC and teacher at Thornhill College.
Conal McFeely: founder of Ráth Mór, chair of St Columb's Hall Trust and director of the Hive Digital Art Studios at Ráth Mór.
Nicholas McGarrigle: poster and programme designer with TC.
Deirdre McGinley: actor with TC in plays including The Loves of Cass McGuire.
Elaine McGovern: actor in Merchant of Venice with TC.
Bernard McGowan: set construction with TC.
Denis McGowan: stage actor with TC, also appeared on screen and in film.
Fionnuala McGowan: musical accompanist with TC, published short-story writer.
Michael McGowan: lead actor and producer with TC and director of the Banba Touring Company. Became head of BBC Radio Foyle and later a two-time Bafta award-winning director.
Noeleen McGrath: actor, producer and artistic director with the Performing Arts Academy.
Agnes McGuinness: prompter with TC.
Danny McGuinness: member of the legendary McGuinness singing family. Acted in Shadow of a Gunman with TC.
Melanie McHugh: actor with TC. Performed in The Prime of Miss Jean Brodie, 1983.
Marion McIhinney: costume design with TC.
Cynthia McKay: talented Londonderry High School actor and stage manager with TC.
Malcolm McKay: sound editor with TC.
Susan McKay: teen actor with LHS. Writer, journalist and documentary maker. Press Ombudsman.
Paul McKeever: musical director, choirmaster, and young actor with TC.
Siobhan McKenna: internationally-acclaimed actor who graced the cover of Life magazine. Twice nominated for Tony awards. Guest starred in a TC production of The Loves of Cass McGuire in 1972. See elsewhere for the full story...
Gary McKeone: teen actor in TC's Maria Marten, before going on to work with Field Day and London's South Bank. Writer, playwright and Director of Literature with Arts Council England.
John McKeown: actor in TC's Rising of the Moon.
Tony McKeown: actor with TC in The Patrick Pearse Motel.
Bob McKimm: long-standing actor and stage manager with TC.
Charles McLaughlin: actor in Stephen D with TC.
Declan McLaughlin: stellar singer, artist, designer, producer, co-founder of the North West Musicians' Collective (subsequently the Nerve Centre), and big help with props for this Derry at Play project.
*Gerry McLaughlin: Co-founder, producer, actor and chair with Theatre Club. Probably its calmest ever director.
Kevin McLaughlin: actor with both TC and 71 Players. Sponsor.
Maria McLaughlin: prompter with TC.
Marilyn McLaughlin (née Frazer): multi-award-winning writer, artist and poet. Regular lead actor with TC.
Monica McLaughlin: actor with TC.
Willie McLaughlin: actor with TC in The Tempest, 1992.
Eugene McLoone: stage manager with TC.
John McLoone: actor, performed in The Quare Fella with TC in 1984.
Paul McLoone: actor with St Columb's DS, TC and Radio Foyle. Phenomenal mimic, voice artist and onetime BBC voice-dubber for censored politicians. Award-winning radio broadcaster and lead singer with The Undertones.
Brian McMahon: teen actor in Stephen D and Maria Marten with TC. Photographer and soundscape artist; Stage Manager with Belfast's Opera House.

Finn McMahon: teen actor in Maria Marten with TC.
Jill McMahon: teen actor in Maria Marten with TC.
Mary McMahon snr: rock of calm in the middle of a sea of drama. Deserves a medal.
Mary Clare McMahon: actor in Maria Marten and Waiting for Godot with TC.
Neil McMahon: singer, production with TC, St Columb's PPU, James MacCafferty and others.
*Seán McMahon: polymath. Actor, director, coach, festival director, mentor, lecturer on Shakespeare, poet, reviewer and author of more than 80 books. The engine room firing the Theatre Club and Derry amateur drama for generations.
Aileen McShane: actor with TC in Stephen D.
Greta McTague: stage and screen actor. Head of drama department at St Cecilia's College, inspiring a generation of Derry Girls. Lead in Maria Marten in the Playhouse Theatre Company's production of Maria Marten.
Siobhan McTernan: stage management with TC.
Martin Melarkey: one of the undisputed leaders of Derry's cultural renaissance over the past 35 years. A music, film, animation and art producer, he was a founding member and mainstay of the North West Musicians' Collective and later founding director of the Nerve Centre and Foyle Film Festival. Head Programmer (Education/Community) for Derry's City of Culture year in 2013, he is currently chief examiner for the Moving Image Arts (GCE) qualifications, taught in more than 80 schools across NI.
Paul Moore (aka Ozzy Paul): late lamented writer, producer and dramatist. Founder of An Nua Theatre Company which worked from the Waterside Theatre and the Playhouse.
Sean Moynihan: voice actor with TC in Suburb of Babylon.
Orla Mulhern: actor with TC. Performed in Hugh Leonard's Summer, 1988.
Brian Mullan: innovative Irish language producer and presenter with BBC Radio Foyle and Ulster. Narrator for Joe Mahon's Seanchaí series screened on BBC2. Notoriously hard-to-beat quiz man.
Cathy Mullan: stage production with TC.
Maire Mullan: costume designer with TC.
Mairead Mullan: originally from Dungannon, became a lead actor with TC for two decades. A hugely talented performer in English or Irish.
Myra Mullan: set design with TC.
Peter Mullan: actor and producer with TC, English and drama teacher at St Columb's. Screen credits include Muintir na Darach (1996) and Seanchaí. Neither Peter nor his wife Mairead were originally from Derry. Peter was friendly with Risteard Mac Gabhann and Gerry at Queen's and moved to Derry as a young teacher in the sixties. Dick and Peter were part of a North West company taking part in an Irish-language drama festival in Tyrone but had been abandoned by one of their female leads. A young Dungannon woman, who was acting in another production, gamely offered to stand in, and while on stage opened a set of French doors only to be confronted with the most 'gorgeous' man she had ever seen in real life. The rest is history.
Tom Mullarkey: award-winning architect who produced the first model of Derry's new civic theatre in the 1970s. Set designer with TC. Poet.
Patrick Mullin: actor with TC.
Mary Murphy: multi-talented lead actor with TC, Faces of Ireland, and on TV and film. Drama coach and mentor. Author and regular broadcaster with BBC Radio Ulster and Radio 4.
Liam Neeson: actor with Rónán Downey in My Dear Palestrina, and in Field Day's debut production, Brian Friel's Translations, at the Derry Guildhall in 1980. Today, Ireland's highest-grossing film star.
David Noble: set designer, programme designer and occasional actor with TC - 'anything that required art'. Taught art at LHS and was a school drama coach and festival judge.
Patricia Noble: choreography with TC.
Reg North: actor with TC in The Long Christmas Dinner, 1977.
Terence O'Brien: actor with TC, university lecturer at Magee then Coleraine.
Matt O'Callaghan: set design with TC.
Brian O'Connor: lead actor and producer with TC. As an architect also proved a most useful set designer. Performed in Streetcar Named Desire in 1988 inter alia.
Pat O'Doherty: stage production with TC.
Paul O'Doherty: TC stalwart in the 1980s. Actor and director, performed in The Quare Fella in 1984.
Austin O'Donnell: actor and singer with TC and St Columb's DS. Died tragically young. The Derry Feis runs a singing cup in his memory.
Bart O'Donnell: St Columb's PPU actor and regular TC lead from his student days.
Colm O'Donnell: actor with TC in The Visit.
Doreen O'Donnell: set designer with TC.
Margaret O'Donnell: actor with TC.
Marie O'Donnell: actor with TC. Performed in The Prime of Miss Jean Brodie, 1983.
Noel O'Donnell: actor, performed in The Quare Fella with TC in 1984.
Michael O'Hagan: actor, performed in The Quare Fella with TC in 1984.
Frank O'Kane: actor and set designer with TC.
Kitty O'Kane: actor with TC. Performed in The Prime

of Miss Jean Brodie, 1983.
Maureen O'Kane: actor in The Visit with TC.
Marie O'Keeney: actor in Plaza Suite with TC in 1985.
Declan O'Kelly: actor and producer with TC.
Mary O'Leary: actor, sets, stage manager and wardrobe mistress with TC.
John O'Neill: guitarist and chief songwriter with the Undertones. Founding member of the Musicians' Collective and Nerve Centre. When he was a young student at the Tech, his mother asked Gerry, who was teaching him English, to tell him to give up his fledgling music career and concentrate on his studies. Gerry, to his eternal credit, said nothing.
Úna Ó Somacháin: director of the MacCafferty School of Music and numerous music festivals. Toured America with the Little Gaelic Singers rubbing shoulders with Elvis, Bing Crosby and Rosemary Clooney. One of the North West's greatest singers and regular performer with Faces of Ireland and TC.
Nonie O'Sullivan: actor with TC in The Queen and the Rebels.
John Page: actor with TC in Shadow of a Gunman and other plays.
Ita Patton: set designer with the '71 Players, Freelance Theatre Company and the Port Pageant.



**Gordon Fulton's production of the Brian Friel classic Philadelphia, Here I Come.**

Jim Patton: hard-working, straight-talking, award-winning director with the '71 Players and Freelance Theatre Company. First-class festival organiser, actor, coach and judge, and producer of Eamon Friel's acclaimed Port Pageant, telling Derry's emigration story. Committee member with the Theatre Action Group.
Monica Pemberton: stage management with TC.
Robin Peoples: actor with TC in Men Without Shadows, 1972.
Terry Phillips: actor, performed in The Quare Fella with TC in 1984.
Connor Porter: multi-talented actor with TC and the Playhouse, tackling everything from romantic leads to Victorian villains. A leading member of the Wednesday Night Arts Appreciation Society, along with Gerry, Joe Mahon, Risteard Mac Gabhann, Dermot Kelly, Ronnie Mullan, Kevin Donohoe, and the late Tom Mullarkey, Peter Mullan and others.
Siobhan Porter: set design with TC.
Lawrence Price: mask designer for TC, The Barber of Seville, 1993.
Stephen Price: ingenious drama producer with Radio Foyle, and actor in Joe Mahon's BBC TV series Seanchaí. Producer and broadcaster with RTE, TV3, Radio Ireland, Radio Ulster and others. Author and historian.
Celine Quigley: publicity with TC.
John Quigley: actor with TC in The Barber of Seville, 1993.
Robert Quigley: actor, performed in The Quare Fella with TC in 1984.
Betty Quinn: prompter with TC.
John Quinn: set designer with Playhouse Theatre Company. Award-winning architect.
Peter Quinn: actor, performed in The Quare Fella with TC in 1984 and with Banba Touring Company.
Gerry Rainey: actor in The Loves of Cass McGuire with TC. Played football with Gerry for Collegians.
Stephen Rea: internationally-acclaimed film and TV actor. Co-founder of Derry's Field Day Theatre Company with Seamus Deane, Brian Friel, Seamus Heaney and Tom Paulin.
Morna Regan: teen player with Thornhill DS and assistant with Field Day. Fulbright Scholar in Theatre, before becoming a professional actor on screen and stage. Irish Times award-winning playwright and IFTA-nominated screenwriter for RTE's Hidden Assets. Rónán Downey's great friend.
Professor Edwin (Ted) Rhodes: Director of the Magee Institute of Continuing Education and its representative on the Theatre Action Group.
George Roddy: costume designer with TC.

Judith Roddy: teenage acting student at St Cecilia's DS and Derry's Foyle Arts Centre. Award-winning stage actor in London, Dublin and New York, with many TV and film credits. Currently starring in Straight Line Crazy with Ralph Fiennes on Broadway.
Neil Roddy: designer par excellence with Colmcille Press and others.
Pauline Ross: writer, producer and founder of the Derry Playhouse. Actor, producer with 71 Players.
Susan Routley: narrator with TC in Lovers (Winners), 1971.
Philippa Russell: lead actor with TC in several productions, frequently alongside her brother-in-law Barney Toal.
Eilish Ryder: actor, stage manager and Club Secretary with the Theatre Club. Roles included: Lucia in The Long Christmas Dinner, 1977; Dame Marten in Maria Marten; and Ellie in The Devil A Saint Would be, 1979.
Sarah Ryder: actor with TC. Performed in The Prime of Miss Jean Brodie, 1983.
Roy Seddon: actor with TC in The Visit.
Paul Shepherd: actor, stage manager and production with TC.
Maurice Simms: actor with TC in The Visit.
Dave Simpson: actor in Rising of the Moon/Stage Management.
Dick Sinclair: cover designer with TC.
*Dinah Sinton: narrator in TC's The Death & Resurrection of Mr Roche, 1970. Teacher of English and Drama at LHS.
A.K. Smith: Londonderry Arts Society representative on the Theatre Action Group.
R.D. (Reggie) Smith: directed Hamlet for the Theatre Club and was a founding member of Derry's Theatre Action Group. A BBC producer, and later a professor in Liberal Arts at Magee College, he was married to Fortunes of War novelist Olivia Manning, who based the character Guy Pringle on him. MI5 files claim that Anthony Blunt recruited Smith as a communist spy in 1938, and the BBC subsequently moved him out of documentaries and into the arts because of this. According to TC players, Smith was extremely popular, capable, a bit eccentric and 'very, very bright', and made no attempt to conceal his socialism. (Every single member of the club who spoke of him smiled as they remembered him.)
Joe Stewart: stage management, lights and sets with TC.
Denzil Stewart: actor and producer with TC. English and Drama teacher at LHS. Festival organiser and judge.
Catriona Stone: actor, stage manager and prompter with TC.
David Sweeney: actor with TC in Stephen D.

**Mairead Mullan ages forty years to play Linda Loman in her husband Peter's production of Death of a Salesman.**

Mary Taylor: publicity with TC.
Noeleen Taylor: actor and stage manager with TC.
Kevin Thompson: actor with TC, including early role in the Merchant of Venice.
Siobhan Tiernan: stage management with TC.
*Barney Toal: founding member, actor, producer and raconteur with TC. Also regular Fear a'Tí with the Faces of Ireland troupe. Consummate performer with many groups. Solicitor for Derry Council by day but entertainer by night (and by birth).
Bernard Toal Jr: teen actor in Stephen D with TC.
Paula Toal: lead actor, playing Meg, in TC production of Lovers (Winners) in 1971.
Chris Trotter: stage management with TC.
K Watson: Londonderry Arts Society representative on the Theatre Action Group.
Noel Willman (1918-1988): Derry-born film/stage actor and theatre director, who studied at Foyle College, before making his debut in a hometown production of The Barretts of Wimpole Street in the early 1930s. Went on to RADA and entered repertory theatre. Won a Tony Award in 1962 for directing the original Broadway production of Man for All Seasons. Also Emmy-nominated for his TV direction of A Lion in Winter.
Terry Willman: talented actor, stage manager and costumes designer with TC and 71 Players.
Paul Wilkins: regular actor with TC. Fellow of Churchill College, Cambridge and award-winning poet. Avid reader, book collector and cruciverbalist, who particularly loved parts where he got to smoke.

[*Performed rehearsed readings as the Theatre Club in 1970.]